WORLD WAR II
WARSHIPS

WORLD WAR II
WARSHIPS

D. J. and H. J. Lyon
Edited by Antony Preston

With a foreword by
Vice Admiral B.B.Schofield CB CBE

Special illustrations by
The County Studio, Coleorton, Leicester

ORBIS PUBLISHING · LONDON

Special Illustrations

Germany
Graf Spee 8
Gneisenau 10
Bismarck 12
Köln 14
Prinz Eugen 15
Friedrich Eckholdt 16
Karl Galster 18
U-47 22
U-64 23
Italy
Conte di Cavour 27
Littorio 28
Pola 31
Giovanni delle Bande Nere 32
Japan
Kaga 36
Hiryu 38
Shoho 40
Zuiho 42
Taiho 44
Shinano 44
Ise 46
Nagato 49
Yamato 50
Chokai 54
Yukikaze 58
I-400 60

Great Britain
Illustrious 64
Indomitable 67
Empire Faith 68
Audacity 68
Hood 70
Warspite 72
Royal Oak 74
Howe 76
Exeter 78
Ajax 80
Penelope 82
Jamaica 84
France
Dunkerque 94
Richelieu 96
Algérie 98
The United States
Lexington 104
Yorktown 106
Wasp 108
Independence 110
Sangamon 112
Mississippi 114
Pensacola 118
Indianapolis 121
Johnston 122
Alan M Sumner 124
Ray 125

Endpapers: The British monitor Roberts
bombards German shore emplacements off
Le Havre on D-Day
Overleaf: The British destroyer Ashanti
Right: The German destroyer Friedrich Ihn

© Orbis Publishing Limited London 1976
Printed in Italy by IGDA, Novara
ISBN 0 85613 220 9

Contents

Foreword	vii
Introduction	2
Germany	6
Capital Ships	8
Cruisers	14
Destroyers	16
Submarines	21
Italy	24
Capital Ships	27
Cruisers	30
Japan	34
Aircraft Carriers	36
Capital Ships	45
Cruisers	53
Destroyers	56
Submarines	59
Great Britain	62
Aircraft Carriers	64
Capital Ships	70
Cruisers	78
Destroyers	86
Submarines	88
France	90
Capital Ships	93
Cruisers	98
The United States	100
Aircraft Carriers	103
Capital Ships	114
Cruisers	118
Destroyers	122
Submarines	125

The American 'Essex'-class fleet carrier Hancock *(background) streams a pall of smoke after being hit by a* Kamikaze *aircraft on 7 April 1945*

Foreword

by Vice Admiral B. B. Schofield CB CBE

The study of warship design is a fascinating subject, especially since hull form, armour, armament, speed and displacement often reveal national characteristics. The Royal Navy, for example, was strongly influenced by Admiral of the Fleet Lord Fisher, a great believer in speed and the big gun, whose name will always be associated with the Dreadnought-type battleship and the less successful battle-cruiser. 'Whoever hits soonest and oftenest will win,' he wrote. His supporter, Admiral Sir Reginald Bacon, put it more colloquially when he quoted the advice an old captain gave to one of his midshipmen: 'Boy, if ever you are dining and after dinner over the wine some subject like politics is discussed when men's passions are aroused, if a man throws a glass of wine in your face, do not throw a glass of wine in his; *throw the decanter stopper!*'.

The story of the naval operations of World War II has been told by a number of writers, and the technical details of the warships themselves have been listed in several publications. But a comparison of these ships' designs and their qualities as fighting vessels has not yet been attempted, so far as I am aware. This book by David and Hugh Lyon under the editorial guidance of Antony Preston – all three of whom are technical experts in the field of naval architecture – is therefore most welcome. It deals with the development of the various types of major warships employed by the chief combatants in World War II, ranging from aircraft carriers down to submarines, and compares their design and performance.

The universal desire to construct bigger and better ships than the enemy reached its climax with the building of the two Japanese battleships *Yamato* and *Musashi*, each displacing at full load 70,320 tons (71,450 tonnes) and carrying a main armament of nine 18-inch (460-mm) guns. The war relegated both the battleship and the cruiser, promoting the aircraft carrier to the position held for so long by the former. But the destroyer emerged with added prestige as the 'maid of all work' of the fleets and performed a multitude of duties, serving as, for example, radar picket, anti-submarine and anti-aircraft screen, and convoy escort. While the introduction of carrier-borne aircraft had a major impact on the conduct of operations, the development of the submarine was equally impressive in the British, German, and United States navies, though less so in those of the remaining combatants. The success gained by aircraft equipped with radar in attacking submarines encouraged the search for a closed-cycle engine capable of operating independently of the atmosphere. This goal was ultimately attained by the Germans with their Walther engine, but too late to take part in the war.

Today we are witnessing changes in warship design undreamt of thirty years ago, but a study of the new ships shows that the basic purpose remains as stated by Fisher. There are lessons to be learned from the past, as the text of this book clearly reveals, and the many illustrations in colour and black-and-white which accompany it enhance the value of this well-researched study. I commend this book to all those whose interest embraces the study of warship design.

B. B. Schofield

Acknowledgments

Photographs
Endpapers and title page Imperial War Museum; page v Imperial War Museum; 1 Bapty; 2–3 US Navy; 4–5 Keystone; 6–7 Ferdinand Urbahns; 9–10 Ferdinand Urbahns; 13 Camera Press; 14 Ferdinand Urbahns; 15 Keystone; 17–19 Ferdinand Urbahns; 20 BN Signal/Foliot; 21 H. le Masson; Keystone; 22 René Dazy; 23 Imperial War Museum; 24–5 Alfredo Zennaro; 26 Imperial War Museum; H. le Masson; 29 Ufficio Storico Fototeca; 30 Signal; 31 Ferdinand Urbahns; 33–35 Ufficio Storico Fototeca; 39–40 Imperial War Museum; 42–3 US Navy; 45 BPC Picture Library; 47–9 Imperial War Museum; 50–1 US Navy; 52 Popperfoto; 53 Camera Press; 55 Fujiphotos; Imperial War Museum; 56–7 Fujiphotos; 57 Fujiphotos; 59 Imperial War Museum; 61 Imperial War Museum; US National Archives; 62–3 Imperial War Museum; 65 H. le Masson; 66–7 Imperial War Museum; 70 Imperial War Museum; 73–4 Imperial War Museum; 77 Imperial War Museum; H. le Masson; 79–81 Imperial War Museum; 82–3 Camera Press; 85–7 Imperial War Museum; 88 Camera Press; 88–9 Fox Photos; 89 Imperial War Museum; 90–1 Museé de la Marine; 92 US1S; 93 US Army; 94–5 Musée de la Guerre; 97 Imperial War Museum; Musée de la Marine; 99 Musée de la Marine; 100–1 US Navy; 102 US Army; 103 H. le Masson; 104–5 Keystone; 106–7 US Navy; 107 US Navy; 108 US1S; 108–9 US Navy; 110 Keystone; 111–13 US Navy; 115 US Navy; 116 US Army; 117 US1S; H. le Masson; 118–20 US Navy; 122–3 Keystone; 126–7 US Navy. All artworks copyright Orbis Publishing Ltd.

Right: A convoy of German escort vessels plough through the Atlantic at the end of a storm

INTRODUCTION

This book about the major warships of the larger navies of the Second World War is restricted to the battleships, aircraft carriers, cruisers, destroyers and submarines of these navies for reasons of space, and not because the escorts, minesweepers, landing craft and coastal forces are not interesting or important. It confines itself to the British Royal Navy, the German, Italian, French, and US Navies and the Imperial Japanese Navy because these were the major fighting navies of the war. Other navies, many of which included interesting types of ships, took part in the war, but it was a comparatively small part, and these navies, such as the Norwegian, Polish, Greek, and Yugoslav, were mainly composed of the smaller types of warship. Other navies, especially those of what was then the British Empire, consisted entirely of the same types of vessel as served in one or more of the largest navies, and therefore need not be considered here.

In September 1939, at the beginning of the war, the Royal Navy was still the largest navy in the world. It was also the oldest of the big navies, and one with an unparalleled history of success and gallantry in action. Despite setbacks and heavy losses the Royal Navy did not let down its great tradition, but it had slipped to second place at the end of the war, not because it had diminished in size (in fact it had grown enormously) but because another navy had grown faster.

The German Navy, reluctantly forced to take on this prestigious giant by Hitler, fought a long, hard and stubborn war, but this second German challenge to Anglo-Saxon seapower fared no better than the first. Ironically it was the arm which the German admirals had ignored, the U-boats, which came nearest to forcing Britain to surrender. Although it had been well equipped with powerful new ships, by the end of the war the German Navy had virtually ceased to exist.

One of the most spectacular naval events of the interwar years was the virtual re-creation of the French Navy, but tragic force of circumstance shattered this fine force. The assaults of enemies and ex-allies and a massed scuttling reduced the French Navy to less than half its former size in the course of the war, without allowing it to make the contribution to victory of which it was capable. The Italian Navy had also been expanded and modernized between the wars. It fought, often gallantly, but with no very great success, and it, too, suffered great losses.

The Japanese Navy had established itself as the third biggest in the world at the end of the First World War. Between the wars it changed from being a navy of foreign-designed warships to one largely consisting of Japanese-designed vessels of considerable originality. After an opening year of war in which she achieved an impressive series of victories against the two

The American destroyer Colahan (DD-658) *comes alongside the battleship* Wisconsin (BB-64). *The flexible refuelling hose can be seen in the foreground, between the barrels of a twin 5-inch (127-mm) gun mounting*

strongest naval powers, Japan was gradually forced onto the defensive. Superior industrial power and resources told against her, and by V-J Day the Japanese Navy and merchant navy had dwindled almost to nothing.

Since the 1920s the United States had the right, under the provisions of the Washington Naval Treaty, to build one-for-one with Britain, though the Royal Navy was still actually slightly larger. However, once America began to put her enormous industrial and economic strength behind the effort of building up her armed services there was little doubt that she would soon outstrip the British. It is to the credit of both sides that the process of transition was

nearly always smooth and friendly. By 1945 the United States Navy had become unchallengeably the world's greatest maritime force.

These are the navies whose ships we shall be discussing. There are two other navies which deserve special mention, one because of its size, though for very few other reasons, the other for its original and excellent ships, as well as a fighting tradition second only to that of the Royal Navy in length and glory.

The Dutch Navy, though small at the outbreak of the war, was the heir to a long and magnificent fighting tradition. It was also responsible for some very fine and intelligent designs. The *Tromp* class of light cruisers were fast, well armed, and perhaps the best answer to the problem of building a vessel midway between the cruiser and the destroyer. The class of Dutch destroyers being built at the outbreak of war (one, the *Isaac Sweers*, was towed away to England when the Germans invaded and was completed there) were at least as effective as the British 'J & K' class of medium destroyers. Dutch submarines were efficient vessels, and were equipped with a primitive form of snorkel. The Dutch were also developing a very effective, if complicated, design of mounting for the Bofors anti-aircraft gun which was well ahead of anything designed elsewhere.

Another navy brought into the war by a German surprise attack, and one which was at first sight more impressive, was that of the Soviet Union. The Soviet fleet included battleships and the largest submarine force in the world, besides large modern destroyers and cruisers. But the Soviet Navy, although it suffered heavy losses, made a minimal contribution to the war: the leadership of the Red Fleet had been weakened by Stalin's purges, and sailors were often used as soldiers to bolster the crucially important struggle on land. Also, despite appearances, the *matériel* of the Soviet fleet was not of the highest quality. The most original and effective designs were the ones developed by the Tsarist navy, ships which by 1941 were too old to be effective. To design impressive-looking modern vessels the Soviets had relied heavily on foreign, particularly Italian, assistance, but the results suffered from crude manufacture and inadequate maintenance. A modern navy is perhaps even more difficult for a newly industrialized nation to create than an air force. The Soviet Union was capable of producing really efficient weapons, as the *T*-34 tank and the Il-2 *Sturmovik* aircraft showed, but it was not until some time after the end of the war that Soviet warships were to show similar qualities.

One general point that should be made very clearly before discussing particular warships is that paper comparisons of designs are often misleading. It is too easy to take a quick look at figures for armament, size, speed and protection and state that one design is 'better' than another. All warship designs are compromises between a whole series of factors, and we can ignore none of them without peril. Seaworthiness

A cruiser's catapult floatplane frames a Douglas Dauntless divebomber and a Yorktown-*class carrier during a sweep between the Marshall and Gilbert Islands on 1 February 1942 as the US Navy begins its counterattack*

is important, and often neglected in considering different designs. The question of how well a particular weapon works and how efficiently it can be directed are as important as the paper characteristics of that weapon, such as calibre and rate of fire.

It is worth bearing in mind that a ship of a given tonnage, unless there is some startling technical breakthrough, can only accommodate so much. If one ship, supposedly of equal tonnage to another, is said to have superior armament, speed or some other necessary quality, we can be sure that it is either deficient in some other respect, or that someone has been cheating somewhere along the line by misquoting statistics; this is particularly true of many of the interwar German and Japanese ships. At this point, we must make some mention of the treaties that had such a great, if temporary, influence on warship design. Immediately after the end of the First World War there was a danger that America and Japan, both feverishly building new and larger types of capital ships in competition with one another, would drag the other naval powers into an unwanted naval race. It was felt that the Anglo-German dreadnought-building race had more than a little to do with the rise in tension which led to war breaking out in 1914, and so a determined effort was made to limit naval armaments by international treaty. After a great deal of international wheeling and dealing the Washington Naval Treaty was signed in 1922; this was amended and reinforced by the London Treaty of 1930. The cumulative effect of these treaties was not only to limit the numbers of each type of major warship each navy should possess (for example Britain, America and Japan were to be allowed to have capital ships in the ratio of 5:5:3), but also their maximum tonnage: 35,000 tons (35,488 tonnes) for battleships, 10,000 tons (10,160 tonnes) for the largest type of cruiser. Armament was restricted to 16-inch (406-mm) for battleships, 8-inch (203-mm) for cruisers. A special and rather artificial way of measuring tonnage was developed for comparing ships built under these treaties, known as 'standard' tonnage.

Of course there was a great deal of cheating over the application of these treaty limitations to the design of ships, often blatant cheating in the cases of the Germans and Japanese, less so with British, American and French designs. Nevertheless the treaties had a very great effect on warship design throughout the interwar years. It was not until the London Naval Treaty of 1936 that most of the limitations were abandoned, and the idea of keeping to some restrictions remained nearly up to the outbreak of war for most powers.

The Second World War was a period of rapid and violent technical and tactical change. Air power was suddenly realized to be vital, and anti-aircraft armament was correspondingly increased. Radar appeared and was adapted to naval use. These and other changes meant that few ships which remained in service during the war stayed unaltered. Many of the major refits which affected the ships will be discussed, but it must be remembered that any warship which was not sunk immediately after commissioning received extra weapons or equipment and extra men to work them.

GERMANY

The German Navy had to be rebuilt almost from scratch between the wars, which was both an advantage and a disadvantage. On the one hand nearly all its ships were new, but, on the other, there had been no continuous improvement on First World War designs. The years of disarmament were years in which German warship design stood still – the only advance being among German designers who continued working on submarines in Finland, Holland and Sweden. For a decade the Germans were not able to advance at a time when other navies were adopting new techniques and weapons. As a result of this, the *Bismarck* was little more than an enlarged and improved version of the last German battleships of the First World War, the *Baden* class – ships which the British had experimented with before sinking, and which had prompted the British to produce much more advanced designs.

Germany, as in the First World War, was faced with adversaries more powerful at sea than herself, enemies who were in a favourable position to block her access to the open sea. But she could choose her own moment to strike against an enemy who had to be prepared all the time, and she could also concentrate on ships of great individual power, rather than building large numbers of inferior ships. On the other hand, Germany always failed to treat the heavy surface ships as the expendable assets they in fact were. This lack of inclination to risk ships was coupled to a certain feeling of inferiority to the Royal Navy. It led to such *débâcles* as the Battle of the Barents Sea on 1 May 1942, when the destroyer escort of an Arctic convoy held off the much more powerful *Hipper* and *Lutzow*. This was the fight which caused Hitler to order the abandonment of big ships as a weapon, a somewhat unfair decision as his directives had helped to create the situation in which the German ships failed to press home their attacks.

Before the war Germany had made astonishingly little effort to develop the arm which offered the best chance of defeating Britain. In 1939 she had only a tiny force of ocean-going U-boats, as her admirals were obsessed by the grandiose 'Plan Z' and hoped to have a huge force of battleships and other large warships by 1944. It was a plan which gave little attention to possible foreign reaction or to the ability of German industry to cope with such a programme of construction; it might have been possible if all other warlike projects had been abandoned.

The Germans have always had a reputation for technical efficiency, and certainly much of their equipment was well designed. There were, however, some amazing lapses, such as the complete failure of the new German torpedoes to work effectively, as discovered during the Norwegian campaign. Other aspects of their ships have been given undue prominence; the armour fitted to the *Bismarck*, for example, was no better than that used in contemporary British or American ships. Perhaps the worst German technical failure during the war, however, was to make less efficient use of scientific advice than the enemy, particularly in the sphere of radar. The concept of operational research, developed by the British and Americans, was totally alien to the thinking of the German High Command. The Allied victory in the vital Battle of the Atlantic owed at least as much to the lead in these fields as it did to the exertions of Allied shipyards in building merchantmen and escorts.

The battle-cruiser Gneisenau *was completed just before the outbreak of war as Germany's second capital ship. She is seen here with her new raked 'Atlantic' bow, which improved her seaworthiness. With the funnel cap, it improved her appearance as well. The sloping top of the main armour belt is clearly visible along the hull. After the alterations* Gneisenau *could be distinguished from her sister* Scharnhorst *by her two catapults, one amidships and one on the after 280-mm gun turret, and by the tripod mainmast stepped against the rear side of the funnel. The main fire control can be seen, one long-base rangefinder on the lower control tower and one on the after superstructure. There is also a shorter rangefinder immediately abaft the bridge, and secondary armament directors in domes on the superstructure. The shield on the bow is typical of German heavy ships, and carries the armorial bearings of her namesake, the great Prussian soldier*

Capital Ships

After the end of the First World War, Germany was left with none of the excellent dreadnoughts of the High Seas Fleet – only a handful of old pre-dreadnoughts, useful for training but little else. She was not allowed to build any warship larger than 10,000 tons (10,160 tonnes), carrying more than 11-inch (280-mm) guns. The intention was to keep the German Navy at the level of the Scandinavian navies, whose largest ships were small armoured vessels with a few heavy guns for coastal defence, known only by courtesy as battleships.

Germany's answer to these restrictions was to produce a new type of warship, called an armoured ship but generally known as a pocket battleship. This type combined the armament of a coastal defence battleship, two triple 280-mm turrets, torpedo tubes and a secondary armament of 150-mm guns, with the hull and protection of an armoured cruiser. A startling innovation was made in the engine room, for diesel engines were used for propulsion; these gave the pocket battleships a greater speed than the battleships of the day (though less than battle-cruisers and cruisers) and a very respectable range (though less than was claimed at the time). Other technical innovations, such as the widespread use of welding, were employed to give some

conviction to the stated weight of 10,160 tonnes, though in fact the laden tonnage was well over half that again.

The three pocket battleships, the *Deutschland* (later renamed *Lutzow*), *Graf Spee* and *Scheer*, caused a furore in naval circles when they first appeared. They seemed to be the perfect type of long-range commerce raider, faster than nearly every ship powerful enough to sink them but strong enough to defeat nearly every warship fast enough to catch them. In fact they were not as formidable as they looked. With only two main turrets it was difficult to split their fire between more than one adversary, which was the *Graf Spee*'s downfall at the River Plate. In addition they were little larger, and not much better protected, than contemporary 8-inch (203-mm) cruisers, but they had the prestige of battleships. Vessels fitted with more 203-mm guns, and with better speed and perhaps better protection, might have proved better investments for Germany. Still, the pocket battleships did worry other navies at the time, and although no other navy copied the ships, much effort was put into devising anti-raider tactics. The Germans considered building improved versions later, but other factors intervened and the designs were never taken very far.

GRAF SPEE
Displacement 12,100 tons (12,294 tonnes) normal, 16,200 tons (16,460 tonnes) full load
Length 616 feet 9 inches (187 m 98 cm)
Beam 71 feet 3 inches (21 m 71 cm)
Draught 19 feet (5 m 79 cm)
Machinery 2-shaft diesel motors, 65,800 shp = 26 knots
Armour belt: 1½ to 4 inches (38–102 mm). decks: ¾ to 2¼ inches (19 to 57 mm). turrets: 5 to 5½ inches (127 to 139 mm)
Guns 6 × 11-inch (280-mm), 8 × 5.9-inch (150-mm), 6 × 4.1-inch (105-mm) AA, 8 × 37-mm AA, 10 × 20-mm AA
Torpedo Tubes 8 × 21-inch (532-mm)
Aircraft 2 (1 catapult)
Launched 30 June 1934 by Wilhelmshaven Dockyard

The 'pocket battleship' Admiral Graf Spee seen just before the war. The 'Seetakt' gunnery radar aerial is visible on the front face of the fire control on the control tower; the use of this radar in the Battle of the River Plate marked the first use of radar in surface action. She was sunk too early to be given the raked bow and funnel cap added to her two sisters. The Heinkel biplane shown on the photograph was replaced at the outbreak of war by an Arado monoplane, as depicted in the illustration below

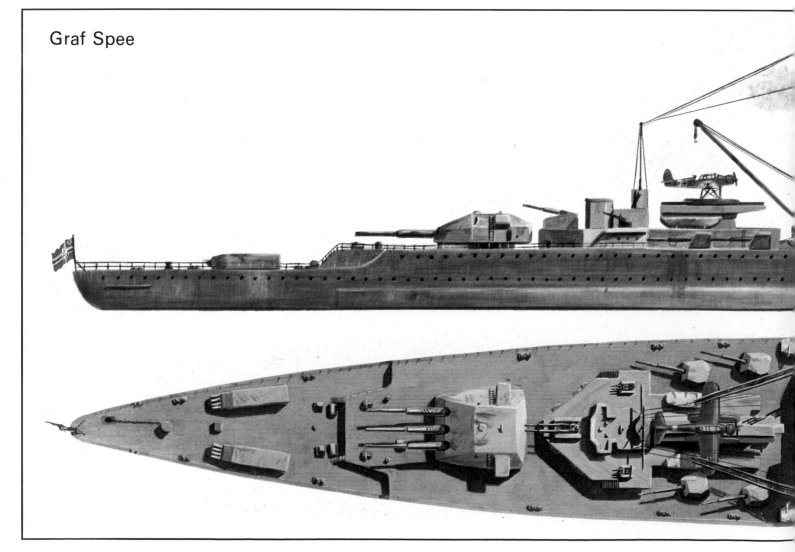

Graf Spee

Gneisenau

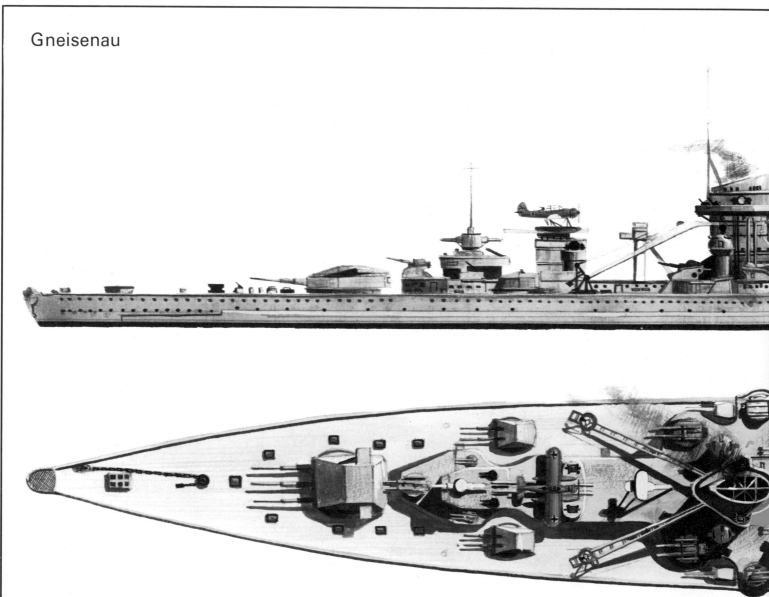

The next German heavy ship design was a much more effective concept. The two armoured ships *Gneisenau* and *Scharnhorst*, like the pocket battleships, caused some problems in classification, some authorities rating them as battle-cruisers, others battleships. Their armour was of battleship standard, but their high speed of 32 knots fitted the battle-cruiser definition better, and their main armament, nine of the same 280-mm guns as the *Graf Spee* and her sisters, was lighter than contemporary battleships. Twin 380-mm guns had been proposed as an alternative to the triple 280-mm, but these turrets were not available when the ships were built. The secondary armament consisted of the same 150-mm guns as in the pocket battleships,

The crew of the Scharnhorst *man the side to sheer the* U-47, *a Type VIIB U-boat. (Under the command of Gunther Prien,* U-47 *penetrated the defences of Scapa Flow in October 1939 and torpedoed the British battleship* Royal Oak.) *At this stage both battleships still had a catapult on the after turret. The drawing below shows* Gneisenau *without the second catapult after wartime modifications*

but the anti-aircraft armament of fourteen 105-mm guns was much heavier. For light anti-aircraft weapons the Germans had the sense to adopt the Bofors design from the start (but using 37-mm ammunition instead of 40-mm) and also the 20-mm heavy machine-gun, well before the Allies did so.

To obtain their high speed these ships adopted steam turbines rather than their predecessors' diesels. Their lack of range was their worst feature, although they made useful sorties against the Allied convoy routes; inadequate bunkers were always a worry, as was also the unreliability of their high-pressure steam installation. Nonetheless, their high speed made them a particular threat to the Allied navies. Even though their armament was inadequate for taking on a battleship, they were still formidable opponents. In the Battle of North Cape on 26 December 1943, in which *Scharnhorst* was finally sunk, it was fortunate for the British that it proved possible to slow her down so the *Duke of York* could engage her, for once this happened she was doomed.

Scharnhorst resembled the pocket battleships, with a straight stem and a flat-topped funnel,

a rather sinister and ugly silhouette. She (and the surviving pocket battleships) were soon, however, altered to look like the *Gneisenau*, which was built with the clipper bow and funnel cap which became the trade mark of the Second World War German heavy ship. This change made them both more handsome in appearance and very difficult to tell apart, a fact which confused the British on several occasions.

GNEISENAU

Displacement 31,800 tons (32,310 tonnes) normal, 38,900 tons (39,524 tonnes) full load
Length 771 feet (235 m)
Beam 100 feet (30 m 47 cm)
Draught 27 feet (8 m 22 cm)
Machinery 3-shaft geared steam turbines, 160,000 shp = 32 knots
Armour belt: 5 to 13 inches (127 to 330 mm). decks: 2 to 4¼ inches (51 to 108 mm). turrets: 9¾ to 14¼ inches (246 to 362 mm)
Guns 9 × 11-inch (280-mm), 12 × 5.9-inch (150-mm), 14 × 4.1-inch (105-mm) AA, 16 × 37-mm AA
Torpedo Tubes 6 × 21-inch (532-mm)
Aircraft 4 (2 catapults)
Launched 8 December 1936 by Deutsche Werke, Kiel

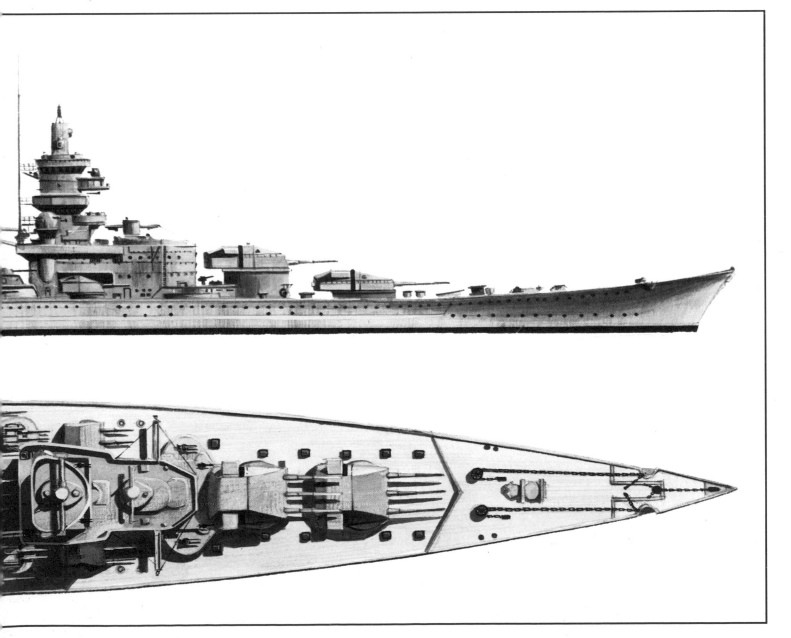

While neither the pocket battleships nor even the *Scharnhorst* and *Gneisenau* were fully equal to foreign battleships, the Germans made a determined effort with the *Bismarck* and her near-sister the *Tirpitz* to produce warships second to none. To a certain extent they succeeded, for these two were certainly impressive in appearance, and had a greater tonnage than any Allied battleships until the American *Iowa* class appeared. Their armour was thick, and they were certainly difficult to sink. However – and this is much more important in a battleship – they were not as difficult to knock out of action as they should have been. As we have already seen, the hull and protection design was basically no more than an enlargement of the quarter-century-old *Baden*, and this gave far too little protection to vital internal communications, particularly as the protective deck was too low.

Though the *Bismarck*'s gunnery against the *Hood* was superb and reaped its reward in the latter's sinking, the *Bismarck* achieved no success at all against *Rodney* and *King George V* on 27 May 1941. After half an hour's pounding, she had not only failed to damage her adversaries, but was a battered wreck incapable of retaliation. After this her sinking was inevitable, and the

argument as to whether it was British torpedoes or a German scuttling party which finally caused her to founder is of very little significance.

For all her size the *Bismarck* was a poor sea boat, and her main armament was no better than older and smaller foreign battleships. A lot of the extra displacement was taken up by having, unlike British and American contemporaries, both a secondary armament of 150-mm guns and a tertiary battery of 105-mm high-angle weapons, instead of a dual-purpose secondary armament. However, the tertiary armament did have the exceptionally good complement of six separate directors (the more directors, the more targets can be engaged at one time, good fire control being more important than number of guns). The light anti-aircraft armament was also excellent for its day.

Tirpitz was basically similar to *Bismarck* except in having greater range and in carrying torpedo tubes. One weakness of the German heavy ships not immediately evident was that their shells had a distressingly high proportion of failures; most of those that hit the *Prince of Wales* in her action against the *Bismarck* and *Prinz Eugen* failed to explode. In the First World War it was the British who were handi-

capped by poor-quality projectiles, whereas in the second conflict it was the Germans who had this trouble.

In short *Bismarck*, though by no means a failure as a fighting ship, was far from being the paragon of excellence she is often claimed to be. If her gunnery had not been so good in the opening minutes of her engagement with the *Hood* it is quite possible that her career might have been even shorter than it was, as the British ship's armour should have proved quite adequate to withstand shelling by the Germans at closer ranges.

Two large battleships to be armed with 406-mm guns were laid down early in the war, but abandoned by the end of 1940. Later battleship and battle-cruiser designs did not develop beyond the project stage, for by that time Germany was sensibly concentrating on U-boat development.

Germany actually launched an aircraft carrier, the *Graf Zeppelin*, and began building another, but the problems of designing this type of ship with no practical experience proved more than the Germans had bargained for. This, combined with the *Luftwaffe*'s hostility to a separate naval air arm, ensured that neither ship was completed.

Bismarck

BISMARCK

Displacement 41,700 tons (42,369 tonnes) normal, 50,900 tons (51,717 tonnes) full load
Length 822 feet 9 inches (250 m 77 cm)
Beam 118 feet 3 inches (36 m)
Draught 29 feet 6 inches (9 m)
Machinery 3-shaft geared steam turbines, 138,000 shp = 29 knots
Armour belt: $12\frac{3}{4}$ inches (323 mm). decks: 2 to $4\frac{1}{2}$ inches (51 to 114 mm). turrets: $12\frac{1}{2}$ to 14 inches (319 to 356 mm)
Guns 8 × 15-inch (380-mm), 12 × 5.9-inch (150-mm), 16 × 4.1-inch (105-mm) AA, 16 × 37-mm AA, 36 × 20-mm AA
Torpedo Tubes none
Aircraft 3 (1 catapult)
Launched 14 February 1939 by Blohm & Voss, Hamburg

The Fuhrer inspects the new battleship Bismarck *in 1941. The radar mattress on the after fire control is clearly visible at top left and the aircraft crane can be seen on the right. The drawing shows how the fixed cross-deck catapult divided the forward and after superstructure. The* Tirpitz *was similar in appearance, apart from having a higher catapult, quadruple torpedo tubes abaft the catapult, and extra anti-aircraft guns*

Cruisers

Köln

The Germans built a number of light cruisers between the wars, apparently more because other navies had examples of the type than for any clearly visualized tactical or strategic purpose. They played an insignificant part in the war. The heavy 203-mm-gun cruisers made more sense, as they would have made good commerce raiders – better than the pocket battleships – had it not been for their short range and machinery troubles.

Among the most interesting of German wartime designs were the *Spähkreuzer* (scout cruisers) designed as escorts for the battleships. Destroyers had proved unable to keep up with the heavy units, so what was basically an enlarged destroyer design was adopted. Several variants were put forward, but the sinking of the *Bismarck* removed any sense of urgency from the programme, and the only one of the class laid down was finally scrapped on the slip.

The first German cruiser built after the First World War, the *Emden*, was completed to a First World War design with single gun mounts, and when she appeared in the mid-1920s she was already obsolescent. The next class, however, consisting of the *Köln*, *Karlsruhe* and *Königsberg*, were well regarded when they were commissioned at the end of the 1920s. They introduced combined diesel and steam-turbine propulsion, which extended their radius of action. But if this was meant to make them useful

as commerce raiders it was wasted effort as they were never employed in that role.

Their layout was quite neat, with three triple 152-mm turrets. The layout aft was unusual in that the two turrets placed there were offset to either side of the centre line. Unfortunately the bridge and forward turret represented too great a concentration of weight forward and the ships did not perform well at sea.

The other two German light cruisers, *Leipzig* and *Nürnberg*, were progressive modifications of the previous design. Both had the two funnels trunked together into a single massive one, triple instead of twin screws, and the after turrets on the centre line. Protection and anti-aircraft armament were both improved, but in terms of results achieved these ships still compared unfavourably with the 152-mm cruisers of all the other major navies.

A class of six light cruisers was proposed early in the war, but of these only three were begun, and these were scrapped on the slips. Their main armament of eight 150-mm guns would have been in twin turrets, they would have had a large mine capacity, and the high speed of 35.5 knots. However, their protection would have been thin and their anti-aircraft armament minimal, so perhaps it is as well that they were never completed.

Unless one counts the pocket battleships as heavy cruisers, Germany did not begin building

The light cruiser Köln *is depicted in her original state with an aircraft and catapult in the drawing. The photograph shows her as later modified with the catapult removed. The* Prinz Eugen *(right) was the last, the luckiest and the best of the German heavy cruisers. The photograph shows her at Boston, USA on her way to take part in the nuclear tests at Bikini in 1946. The wreck was scuttled at Kwajalein a year later – a sad end for a fine ship*

KOLN
Displacement 6,650 tons (6,756 tonnes) standard, 8,350 tons (8,484 tonnes) full load
Length 570 feet 9 inches (173 m 96 cm)
Beam 50 feet 3 inches (15 m 31 cm)
Draught 17 feet 9 inches (5 m 41 cm)
Machinery 2-shaft geared steam turbines and diesels, 68,000 shp + 1,800 bhp = 32 knots
Armour belt: 2 inches (51 mm). deck: $\frac{3}{4}$ inch (18 mm). turrets: $1\frac{1}{4}$ inches (30 mm)
Guns 9 × 6-inch (152-mm), 6 × 3.5-inch (88 mm) AA, 8 × 37-mm AA, 4 × 20-mm AA
Torpedo Tubes 12 × 21-inch (532-mm)
Aircraft 2 (1 catapult)
Launched 23 May 1928 by Wilhelmshaven Dockyard

ships of this kind until the mid-1930s, just when the Royal Navy was abandoning the type. Three were completed for the German Navy, *Hipper*, *Blücher* and *Prinz Eugen*, while another was sold to the Soviets and a fifth began to be converted to an aircraft carrier but was never completed. *Blücher* was sunk by Norwegian shore defences before she was even fully worked up, *Hipper* had constant and chronic machinery trouble, while *Prinz Eugen*, which was a slightly improved version of the other two, was the most successful of the class.

Like all of the earlier heavy units *Hipper* was completed with straight stem and flat-topped funnel, but was later converted to resemble her sisters with clipper bow and funnel cap. All three were powerful vessels with a strong secondary armament, good speed and much heavier pro-

tection than any of the other European 8-inch (203-mm) cruisers except the *Algerie*, which was their only equivalent in the British and French navies.

They were excellent ships apart from their unreliable high-pressure boilers and the poor action radius given by their steam turbines. Perhaps a few of the anti-aircraft guns could have been given up for extra fuel tanks, and certainly better range would have made these ships excellent raiders. For they, much more than the pocket battleships, were fitted to outrun anything stronger and crush anything faster. *Prinz Eugen*, in fact, played a very creditable part in supporting the *Bismarck* against the *Hood* and *Prince of Wales*; her 203-mm guns were obtaining hits even before the 380-mm guns of the *Bismarck*, and her silhouette confused the

British ships into diverting their fire onto her. The only disappointment is that she achieved nothing after separating from her larger consort, apart from escaping to France.

PRINZ EUGEN
Displacement 14,800 tons (15,037 tonnes) normal, 19,800 tons (20,117 tonnes) full load
Length 689 feet (210 m)
Beam 71 feet 6 inches (21 m 79 cm)
Draught 19 feet (5 m 79 cm) mean
Machinery 3-shaft geared steam turbines, 132,000 shp = 32 knots
Armour belt: $3\frac{1}{4}$ inches (82 mm). decks: $1\frac{1}{4}$ to $2\frac{1}{2}$ inches (30 to 63 mm). turrets: $6\frac{1}{2}$ inches (164 mm)
Guns 8 × 8-inch (203-mm), 12 × 4.1-inch (105-mm) AA, 12 × 37-mm AA, 8 × 20-mm AA
Torpedo Tubes 12 × 21-inch (532-mm)
Aircraft 3 (1 catapult)
Launched 22 August 1938 by Germania Yard, Kiel

Prinz Eugen

Destroyers

At the end of the First World War the Germans had just begun building a class of very large destroyers armed with 150-mm guns. Although not particularly successful (the weapons were really too large and clumsy for the type of ship) the design was influential. The Italians and French each incorporated one example in their navies, and proceeded to produce their own 'super destroyer' designs shortly afterwards. In fact, except perhaps for specialized raiding purposes in the Mediterranean, the British answer – larger numbers of smaller and cheaper destroyers supported by cruisers – made much more sense. Even the largest destroyer was no match for a small cruiser, and one of the most important aspects of the destroyer type was that it was the largest type of warship which could easily be considered expendable. The 'super destroyers' were getting too large and expensive to come within this definition.

At first the Germans very sensibly stuck to building modernized versions of their small destroyers of 1914–18. Called 'torpedo boats', these were quite adequate for use in the narrow seas in which the German Navy would normally have to operate. But by the mid-1930s Germany decided to return to building large destroyers.

The first class of large destroyers, Z 1 to Z 16, (they were all given names as well as numbers) would have been excellent ships if they had been more seaworthy, and if it had not been for trouble with their unreliable high-pressure steam machinery installation. Their armament of five 127-mm guns in a similar layout to American and French contemporaries was sensible, and their ten torpedo tubes would have made them formidable adversaries early in the war had it not been for the failure of German torpedoes at that stage. Thanks to the German adoption of the 37-mm gun their anti-aircraft equipment was better than British contemporaries, but the much smaller British ships could fight them on equal terms by themselves, and if in difficulties could summon up heavy support. This rendered pointless the German attempt to meet numbers with superior quality, as the appearance of HMS *Warspite* at the Second Battle of Narvik on 13 April 1940 showed.

Perhaps the most effective use of these German destroyers was as fast minelayers in 1939–40, a task they performed well and with considerable results. The few which survived the Battle of Narvik underwent the usual modifications to fit more light anti-aircraft guns in the course of the war, often losing one of their 127-mm guns to preserve stability.

Unfortunately, despite the fact that this class of destroyers were nearly the size of former light cruisers, they proved inadequate for this purpose, particularly in the northern waters where they spent so much of the war. They are fine examples of how the lack of attention to purely 'ship' qualities can detract from the performance of a warship as a weapon system.

Despite their size, German destroyers nearly always came off worst when they met cruisers. The *Z 16* was no exception. She was part of a force of destroyers which was supposed to be screening the *Hipper* and *Lützow* during the Battle of the Barents Sea, but which was detached from the heavy ships to little real purpose while a convoy protected by the smaller British

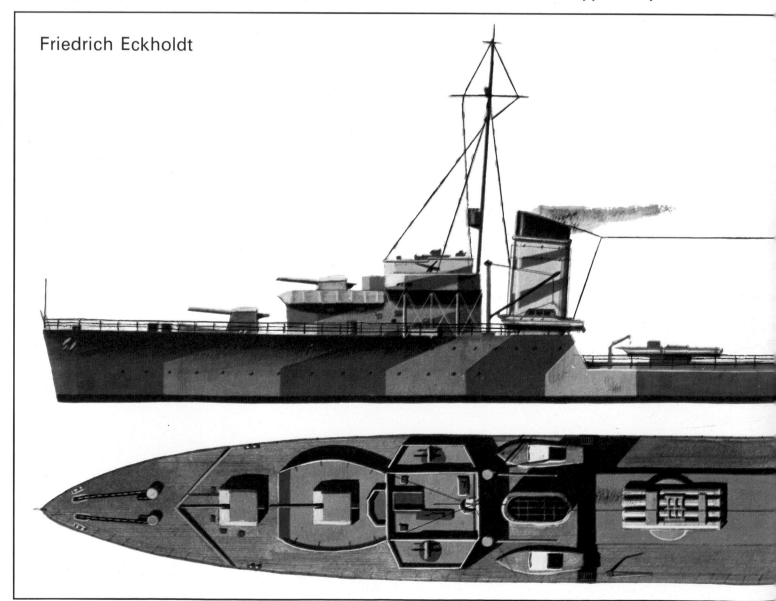

Friedrich Eckholdt

destroyers was defending itself with gallantry and success. Suddenly, two larger vessels appeared indistinctly through the murk of a northern winter's day. *Z 16* attempted to join these two, presuming they were friendly. She was overwhelmed by the 6-inch (152-mm) guns of the *Sheffield* and *Jamaica* who were rushing to the convoy's assistance.

FRIEDRICH ECKHOLDT

Displacement 2,239 tons (2,274 tonnes) normal, 3,165 tons (3,215 tonnes) full load
Length 397 feet (121 m)
Beam 37 feet (11 m 27 cm)
Draught 12 feet 6 inches (3 m 80 cm)
Machinery 2-shaft geared steam turbines, 70,000 shp = 38 knots
Armour none
Guns 5 × 5-inch (127-mm), 4 × 20-mm AA
Torpedo Tubes 8 × 21-inch (532-mm)
Launched 21 March 1937 by Blohm & Voss, Hamburg

A pre-war view of the ill-fated destroyer Friedrich Eckholdt (Z 16). *The number on her side is the flotilla number*

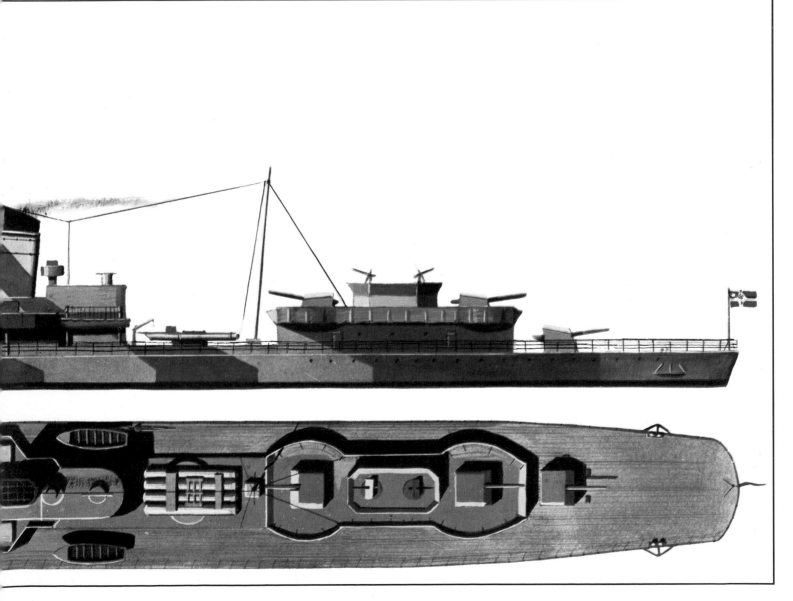

The next class of German destroyers (*Z 17–Z 22*) were slightly lengthened to improve seaworthiness. More effective, however, in achieving this aim was the clipper bow which replaced the straight stem in the *Z 20* and the two other later members of the class. This was their only real difference from their predecessors, as no effort had been made to improve the reliability of the machinery. Despite the setting up of a committee before the war to investigate the deplorable frequency of boiler breakdowns, no real answer was found, and so throughout the war these destroyers had to be carefully 'nursed' by their engineers. It was rare to find all boilers serviceable at any one time.

Most of the German destroyers were sunk during the war; *Z 20* was one of the few exceptions. Three of the survivors were taken into the French Navy, several temporarily joined the Royal Navy, and *Z 20*, like a couple of her sisters, went to the Soviet Union.

Most of the remaining German destroyers completed during the war were fitted with 150-mm guns instead of 127-mm. One, the *Z 28*, was fitted as a leader, and only had four guns because of her extra accommodation. The others were all designed to have twin guns in a turret forward and the other three in single mounts aft, but because of delays in the delivery of the twin turret most of these ships only had a single gun forward at first. Once the turrets were fitted they were found to be very unsatisfactory; they were far too heavy, and the concentration of weight forward naturally reduced seaworthiness and strained the ship. German destroyer captains were soon comparing this mounting unfavourably with the far lighter and much more satisfactory British twin destroyer mounts. Despite the complaints, the twin turret was retained. It was the foremost of the single guns mounted aft which was removed when the time came to lighten the ship to take extra anti-aircraft weapons.

It is obvious that the 150-mm gun was not really suitable as a destroyer weapon, being too heavy and clumsy to operate on a small ship and adversely affecting seaworthiness and structural strength. It is therefore not surprising that the last German destroyers to be completed before the surrender reverted to 127-mm guns in the original single-mounting layout.

Those ships had not changed much in appearance or design from their predecessors. Some considerably altered designs were begun, though not completed, one introducing a new twin 130-mm dual-purpose turret, of which it was to have had three. A single experimental diesel-powered destroyer was being built and the final class to be laid down combined the new weapon with diesel propulsion and an impressively large anti-aircraft armament.

KARL GALSTER

Displacement 2,411 tons (2,449 tonnes) normal, 3,415 tons (3,469 tonnes) full load
Length 410 feet (124 m 96 cm)
Beam 38 feet 9 inches (11 m 81 cm)
Draught 12 feet 6 inches (3 m 80 cm)
Machinery 2-shaft geared steam turbines, 70,000 shp = 38 knots
Armour none
Guns 5 × 5-inch (127-mm), 4 × 37-mm AA
Torpedo Tubes 8 × 21-inch (532-mm)
Launched 15 June 1938 by AG Weser, Bremen

Like most of the earlier German destroyers, the Karl Galster had a number (Z 20) as well as a name. She was the only one of her class to survive the war, as the remaining five were sunk at Narvik. The illustrations show how little this class differed from Z 1 to Z 16. Wartime destroyers differed little in basic design and appearance

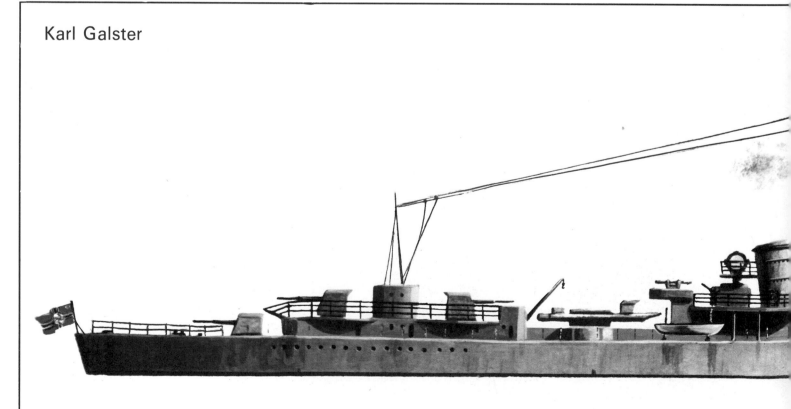

Karl Galster

Submarines

The Germans were more successful in keeping a certain continuity in the design of submarines after the end of the First World War than they were with any other type of vessel. This is one of the reasons why the U-boats were the most satisfactory of all German warship types. The other eminently successful and well-designed German warship type, the *S-Boat* or MTB ('E-Boat') should not be ignored, even though space does not permit any description of them.

Submarines were the only type of ship in which the German Navy of the First World War had outnumbered the Royal Navy. There was variety, too, in the German submarine fleet; besides the medium-sized vessels which she had continued to develop throughout the war, Germany had the large 'U-cruisers' armed with 150-mm guns and capable of crossing the Atlantic, the small minelayers of the 'UC' classes, and the coastal boats of the 'UB' group, which started small, but evolved into a design which was to be the basis of the standard Second World War U-boat. With the end of the First World War, Germany lost all these submarines, but the teams which designed them were kept at work in exile in other countries – Finland, Spain, Holland and Sweden. Germany was not allowed to have any submarines until 1934, but her designers were ready with improved versions of vessels built abroad for foreign navies, which themselves were in a direct line of descent from the best First World War designs. Fortunately for Britain, full advantage was not taken of the opportunity to build these boats before the war. German admirals were dreaming grandiose dreams of super-battleships and gave little thought to the building or use of the one type of vessel that could win the war for them, if used in sufficient numbers and with adequate skill. The U-boats did remarkably well in the early part of the war, though handicapped by the failure of their over-complicated and insufficiently developed torpedoes. During the period from 1941 to 1943, when the deficiencies in both torpedoes and submarine numbers had been overcome, the U-boats came close to winning. However, as time went on the sheer quantity of Allied shipbuilding production began to tell, and, more important, the Allies began to win the scientific battle. New types of radar were developed, ahead-throwing weapons like 'Hedgehog' and 'Squid' made surface escorts more deadly, and rockets and acoustic homing torpedoes did the same for aircraft. One of the most effective weapons against U-boats was their own radio chatter with their bases, used by Allied ships to track them down.

It was not that the U-boats did not have new weapons of their own, such as homing and pattern-running torpedoes, decoys like the '*pillenwerfer*' to give false echoes on Asdic, radar detectors, and extra 20-mm guns to turn the boats into flak traps for Allied aircraft. Despite all these, the U-boats were overwhelmed and by

Left: Type VIIC U-boat on patrol in the Pacific; this version was to be replaced by the Type XXI. Right: Incomplete Type XXI hulls at Bremen and a scuttled VIIC and XXI in dry dock

the end of 1943 decisively defeated in the chief battleground, the North Atlantic. The number of skilled commanders and crews on the German side dropped, whereas the Allies' experience and skill grew. Right at the end of the war the Germans were ready to attempt a comeback with radically new designs of submarine, but they were far too late. The *Schnorkel* had been brought into use rather earlier and gave the U-boats a greatly extended range underwater, but it was essentially a defensive innovation, whose use helped to prevent U-boats being sunk but was of little good in assisting them to sink enemy ships.

The first submarines built for the *Kriegsmarine* were the Type I, ocean-going boats based on a design built in Spain for Turkey, of which only two were built, and the Type II, small coastal boats of more use for training than anything else.

The mainstay of German submarine building throughout the war was the next design to appear, the Type VII. These were developed, via a Finnish boat, from the later First World War 'UB' boats. The Type VIIs were the smallest possible design for ocean going, well armed and with a good diving performance. The Type VIIB version (of which the *U-47* which sank the *Royal Oak* was one) was a slightly improved version of the original Type VIIA. They were slightly bigger and more seaworthy, and had more powerful diesels. The VIIC which followed was improved by the addition of extra torpedo reloads and a better light anti-aircraft

armament, but was otherwise unchanged. This design became the standard production version, and was built in greater numbers than any other submarine type. The concomitant of this was that, by the end of the war, more vessels of this type had been lost in action than of any other warship class at any time or anywhere. They had, however, also achieved a similarly record number of merchant ships (and a fair number of warships) sunk.

As the war went on, design alterations were made on the stocks and during refits. More 20-mm and 37-mm guns were added, usually with the removal of the 88-mm deck gun. Some 'Flak-Trap' U-boats carried an impressive total of these automatic cannon in an attempt to discourage the increasingly deadly long-range anti-submarine aircraft the Allies were using. This was, in the event, a mistaken move; U-boats which stayed on the surface to fight it out were liable to be kept there till the aircraft that found them had summoned other aircraft, or even warships, to make a concerted attack. After numbers of U-boats had been lost in this way the experiment was abandoned.

The *Schnorkel* was more successful, but only appeared towards the end of the war, when it gave some respite to the battered survivors of the defeat in the battle of the convoys. Later models of the Type VII were given stronger hulls to increase the already impressive maximum diving depth. This was greater for German boats than for other nations' submarines. The Type VIID minelaying version had an extra section

fitted with vertical mine tubes abaft the conning tower. The Germans and French preferred these vertical tubes for minelaying, but the British and Americans preferred rails laid on top of the pressure hull and covered by a casing, laying the mines through ports in the stern. The VIIF design also had an extra section added amidships, but this time to carry extra torpedoes.

The variants of the Type VII had been extremely successful designs in their day, but by the end of the war they had become obsolete and were easy meat for their opponents. They were also small for oceanic warfare, and, though this gave them excellent underwater manoeuvrability, important in the evasion of depth charge attacks, it also meant that the crews lived in badly cramped conditions.

U-47
Displacement 753 tons (765 tonnes) surfaced, 857 tons (870 tonnes) submerged
Length 218 feet 3 inches (66 m 52 cm) waterline
Beam 20 feet 3 inches (6 m 17 cm)
Draught 5 feet 6 inches (1 m 67 cm)
Machinery surfaced: 2-shaft diesel-electric, 2,800 bhp = $17\frac{1}{4}$ knots. submerged: 2-shaft electric, 750 shp = 8 knots
Guns 1 × 3.5-inch (88-mm), 1 × 20-mm AA
Torpedo Tubes 5 × 21-inch (532-mm)
Launched 29 October 1938 by Germania Yard, Kiel

Two main types of U-boats fought the Battle of the Atlantic. U-47 (below) a Type VIIB, was developed into the standard workhorse Type VIIC while the larger, long-range Type IXB (right) patrolled more distant waters

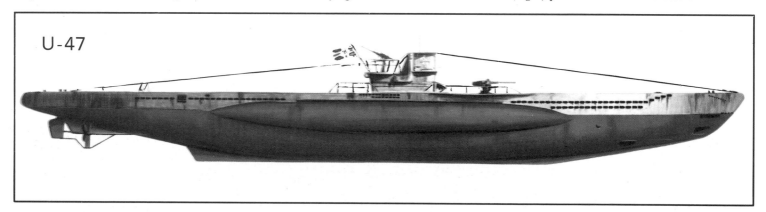

U-47

The Type VIIs also had insufficient endurance for the longer patrols which were necessary in a world war. The larger and longer-range German standard production type developed to fill this gap was the Type IX. This traced its ancestry through the Type I (of which it was an enlargement), via the Spanish-built Turkish *Gür* to the *U-81* class of the First World War.

The initial group, the Type IXA, carried an impressive number of reloads for their six tubes, 22 torpedoes in all, or could carry mines instead. The Type IXB was merely a similar design with improved bunkerage and therefore increased radius, while the next development, the IXC, was further improved in this respect. These larger and clumsier boats were, in general, not as popular with their crews as the Type VIIs, but were in fact the most successful of all U-boats in the total of merchant ship tonnage sunk per submarine.

The first two of the IXD type were special cargo submarines, designed for communicating with Japan and capable of carrying small quantities of certain vital commodities. Their engine installation was designed for a high surface speed, but proved unsatisfactory and had to be replaced. The second type of IXD was also designed for operation in distant seas, but was armed with torpedoes (with an alternative mine armament if required).

The Type XBs (Type XA was a design that was never built) were large minelayers, fitted with only a couple of stern tubes and a defensive gun armament in addition to their 66 mines, in external and internal vertical tubes. They were more often used as supply boats to extend the endurance of other boats than for minelaying.

The role of 'Milch Cow' submarine tankers and supply boats gained greater importance as Allied successes in the North Atlantic drove the U-boats further afield in search of easier pickings, a search which proved delusive. A special type of submarine tanker, the Type XIV, was therefore developed. These ships had shorter and fatter hulls, though much the same tonnage as the IXDs. They were comparatively easy targets, and thanks to good intelligence many of them were caught and sunk, particularly by US escort carriers operating in the South Atlantic.

Towards the end of the war, Germany made giant strides in submarine design and produced boats which were true submarines designed to operate almost entirely below the surface, instead of being submersibles intended chiefly for surface operations and brief dives. This was done by streamlining the hull for underwater speed, providing greatly increased battery power for high and sustained underwater speed, and *Schnorkels* for recharging the batteries. The larger versions of this new concept were known as the Type XXI, and a smaller coastal version was the Type XXIII. Both types made extensive use of prefabrication, and some that were completed were useless because of this.

The Germans also made many experiments with the closed-circuit Walther hydrogen peroxide turbine system, theoretically ideal for submarines, but the building of a series of type XVIIA and B boats powered entirely by these turbines, and others with combined diesel and hydrogen peroxide propulsion, was premature. Even after the war, when the British built a couple of submarines on this system and made many experiments, the turbines never worked completely satisfactorily. The Germans put much energy into a whole series of other diverse projects, such as closed-circuit diesel submarines and many other fascinating designs, but one cannot help feeling that this was a mistaken diversion of resources.

U-64
Displacement 1,051 tons (1,068 tonnes) surfaced, 1,178 tons (1,197 tonnes) submerged
Length 251 feet (76 m 50 cm)
Beam 22 feet 2 inches (6 m 76 cm)
Draught 15 feet 4 inches (4 m 70 cm)
Machinery surfaced: 2-shaft diesel, 4,400 bhp = $18\frac{1}{4}$ knots. submerged: electric motors, 1,000 shp = $7\frac{1}{4}$ knots
Guns 1 × 4.1-inch (105-mm), 1 × 37-mm AA, 1 × 20-mm AA (a second 20-mm gun was later added, and in some cases one quadruple and two twin 20-mm mounts or one 37-mm AA and two 20-mm AA mounts)
Torpedo Tubes 6 × 21-inch (532-mm), four bow, two stern
Launched 20 September 1939 by AG Weser, Bremen

Below left: The Type II was the most numerous U-boat type at the beginning of the war.
Below: U-883, a Type IXD2, lies alongside three Type VIIC boats after the surrender at Wilhelmshaven

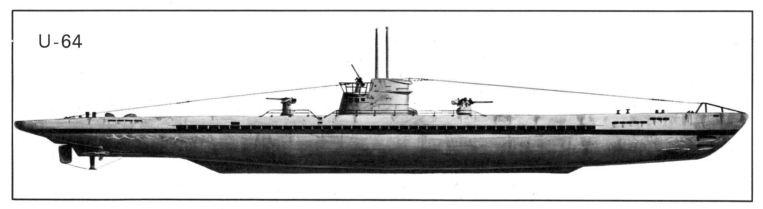

U-64

ITALY

Until the Allied invasion of North Africa in November 1942, the Italian Navy was on paper the strongest in the Mediterranean, but its major units suffered an almost uninterrupted run of defeats. The reasons for this did not lie in the quality of the ships; despite an emphasis in some vessels on speed almost to the exclusion of all else, the general standard of design was high. Nor did the fault lie in a lack of individual courage and ability; in the use of specialized small craft and frogmen (which there is not room to deal with here), the Italian Navy showed skill and daring second to none. The failure lay chiefly with the politicians and the Italian Navy's High Command.

As in the First World War, unwillingness to accept losses resulted in timorous use of heavy units, and as a result they were unable to achieve the results that they were capable of. Apart from a weakness in the underwater protection of the battleships and heavy cruisers, and a lack of radar till late on in the war, there were no design faults that justified this timidity. Other navies achieved more with less. The smaller units of the Italian fleet, not dealt with in this book, were often equipped with vessels whose designs were no better than the heavy units, and this particularly applied to the anti-submarine forces, yet the results they achieved were more impressive

because they were used courageously and imaginatively. If the battle fleet and submarines had been used like the small units, there was no reason why the Italians, even without aircraft carriers, should not have completely controlled the central Mediterranean. With carriers they could have swept the sea bare of Allied vessels.

When Italy entered the war on 10 June 1940, hers was the only major navy with no aircraft carriers in service or under construction. At a meeting of the senior admirals chaired by Benito Mussolini in December 1925 it had been confirmed that Italy should not build carriers, as it was felt that land-based aircraft operating from the Italian peninsula would be able to provide any support necessary. After a series of

actions, culminating in the Battle of Cape Matapan on 28 March 1941 in which the British use of carriers had shown their worth and the Italian Air Force had been unable to provide the expected support, the Italians decided to convert two 30,500-tonne liners, *Roma* and *Augustus*, into carriers as soon as possible. They were renamed *Aquila* and *Sparviero* respectively. Using some equipment from the German *Graf Zeppelin*, and with the help of German engineers, *Aquila* was almost ready for sea trials at the time

of the armistice. Neither ship was ever completed, and both were eventually scuttled.

The first Italian interwar destroyers, the *Leone* class, were large (1,770 tonnes) and heavily armed (eight 120-mm guns and four 530-mm torpedo tubes) and were originally classed as scouts. The next three classes were half the size, and were fast but otherwise undistinguished. The next class of large destroyers were the twelve *Navigatori* vessels, the first of which were laid down in 1929 and which were at first also classified as scouts. With a designed speed of 38 knots instead of the 34 knots of the *Leone* class and an armament of six 120-mm guns and four to six 530-mm torpedo tubes, these ships were built as an answer to the early French *Contre Torpilleurs*. They were poor sea-boats, and before the war most had their bows heightened in an attempt to improve this. The considerably smaller *Dardo* class (1,220 tonnes) were also laid down in 1929 and became the basis of subsequent Italian destroyer development, with single funnel, very high speed, and an armament of four 120-mm guns and six 530-mm torpedo tubes. They were followed by the very similar *Folgore* class and the somewhat larger *Maestrale* and *Oriani* classes. Then came the 1,830-tonne *Soldati* class, built between 1937 and 1942. There were twelve in the first group, and seven (of which two were

never completed) in the second, which had five 120-mm guns. This proved a successful and useful design.

Early in 1943, a new class of large destroyers, the *Commandanti Medaglie d' Oro,* with an armament of four 135-mm guns, were laid down but none were ever completed.

In addition to their gun and torpedo armament, all Italian destroyers were fitted for minelaying.

Italian destroyer development in the 1930s makes an interesting contrast with the French. Whereas the French virtually ignored light cruisers until nearly the end of the decade, and instead built a number of ultra-large very fast destroyers with some slower medium-sized destroyers to escort the fleet, the Italians, until the very end of the decade, built a number of light, fast cruisers and very fast medium-sized destroyers that could perform escort work. In both navies an excessive emphasis was laid on speed, and not enough on other equally valuable attributes.

As with the German and French navies, the Italians also employed a number of fast light destroyers, or torpedo boats, of between 600 and 900 tonnes. Some of these, the *Pilo, Sitori, La Masa* and *Palestro* classes, dated from the First World War, while the first ships of the last class to be built, the *Ariete,* were not laid down until 1942.

With 104 submarines in service in September 1939, the Italian Navy had the strongest effective submarine force in the world, and by June 1940 more submarines had been added to the force. Yet it was not until a handful of German submarines entered the Mediterranean in the second half of 1941 that Axis submarines gained any significant successes there.

Once again, it was not the designs that were at fault but the way in which the vessels were used. The best Italian submarine commanders

were moved to Bordeaux to assist the Germans in the Atlantic, and most of the remainder did very little useful work. The most serious design fault general to Italian submarines was the relatively slow emergency diving speed, which made them more vulnerable on the surface than their British counterparts.

The Italians sensibly avoided excessive size, speed, or armament, and their interwar submarines fell into two main types: those of between 1,000–1,500 tonnes surface displacement, having a surface speed of around 17 knots and armed with 120-mm or 100-mm guns and six or eight 530-mm torpedo tubes, and those of between 600 and 800 tonnes surface displacement, with six or eight 530-mm torpedo tubes, 102-mm or 100-mm guns, and a surface speed of between 14 and 17 knots.

The first class of large submarines, the *Balilla* vessels, were laid down in 1925. These were followed in 1926 by *Ettore Fieramosca*, which was designed to carry a small aircraft. Although a hanger was fitted, no aircraft was actually carried until 1931. Then came two classes of somewhat smaller submarines, the *Archimede* and the *Glauco* types. Two of the former were transferred to Spain in 1937, while the latter (originally ordered by Portugal, which later cancelled the contracts) were used by the Italian Navy. Four members of the next three classes, the *Calvi, Marcello* and *Cappellini* groups, were converted into transport sub-

The Italian battleship Littorio *at speed. The tightly bunched anti-aircraft guns amidships were characteristic of Italian battleships, and the high command of the after 380-mm turret was unique to the class. The unusually wide sloping top of the armour belt was produced by the shape of the Pugliese underwater protection. Littorio's fascist name was changed to* Italia *after the armistice in 1943*

marines in 1943 to ship high-value material to and from Japan.

In 1936 the first of the *Brin* class were laid down, two of which were transferred to Spain in 1937. The *Brin* submarines mounted one 100-mm gun in a turret at the aft end of the bridge. The next three classes, the *Luizzi*, *Marconi*, and *Cagni* vessels, were not completed until after Italy declared war. Four of them were later converted into transport submarines. The *Cagni* group, the largest armed submarines built for the Italian Navy, were specially designed for commerce raiding, and had 450-mm torpedo tubes, so as to be able to carry a large number of torpedoes. The last class of large Italian submarines was the 'R' class, armed only with 20-mm guns and intended to be large capacity transports for the Japan run. Only two of these were completed.

The first large minelayer, *Pietro Micca*, was laid down in 1931, and the three *Foca*-class vessels were laid down in 1936. These latter had a 100-mm gun mounted as in the *Brin* submarines, and could carry 36 mines. The two members of the considerably smaller *Bragadin* class, laid down in 1927, could only carry 16 to 24 mines, depending on the type.

The medium-sized *Mameli*-class submarines were laid down in 1925, and were followed between 1925 and 1928 by the *Pisani* and *Bandiera* classes. Both of these lacked stability, and both had later to be fitted with bulges which reduced the surface speed from about 17 to nearly 15 knots, and the submerged speed from nearly 9 to just over 8 knots. These and the succeeding *Squalo* class were all over 800 tonnes surface displacement, but the next class, the *Argonauta* vessels, only displaced just over 600 tonnes on the surface. This class had four different makes of engines. *Jalea* and *Jantina* had Fiat diesels and CRDA electric motors, *Salpa* and *Serpente* had Tosi diesels and Marelli electric motors, and *Argonauta*, *Fisalia*, and *Medusa* had CRDA diesels and electric motors.

The two somewhat larger submarines of the *Settembrini* class were followed by the 12 *Sirena*,

10 *Perla* and 17 *Adua*-class submarines. Two of the *Perla* class, *Ambra* and *Iride*, and two of the *Adua* class, *Gondar* and *Scire*, were modified in 1940–42 to carry, in the case of *Ambra*, *Gondar* and *Scire* three, and *Iride* four, cylinders to transport human torpedoes, the 'Maiale' or 'pigs', best known for the attack on the British battleships *Queen Elizabeth* and *Valiant* in Alexandria harbour in 1941. These cylinders were carried externally on the hull fore and aft of the conning tower.

The *Argo* and the *Valella*, originally laid down in 1931 and finally completed in 1937, were, like the larger *Glauco* submarines, ordered by Portugal which later cancelled the contract. All the 13 vessels of the *Acciaio* class were completed by mid-1942, but only eight of the first series of the *Flutto* class were completed, and several of these were scuttled after the armistice, only having been in service for a month or so. *Pietro Calvi* (ex-*Bario*), which was finally completed to a much modified design in 1961, was the sole member of the second series of the *Flutto* class to see service, out of the 15 that were laid down.

The oldest submarines in service in the Italian Navy in 1940 were the five surviving 'H' class vessels, built in Canada in 1916–17 to the same design as the British 'H' class. These were used exclusively during the war for anti-submarine

training, but in a way they were more valuable to the Italians than their operational submarines, for the Italian anti-submarine forces were extremely good, and managed to sink a large number of Allied submarines.

In addition, the Italians built or planned a number of very small and midget submarines of the 'CA', 'CB', 'CC' and 'CM' types. *CA 2*, in service in 1938, was modified in 1942 to be carried in a specially fitted deck housing on the *Marconi*-class submarine *Leonardo Da Vinci* against American east coast harbours, but the project was eventually abandoned. These vessels make an interesting comparison with their contemporary Japanese and slightly later British and German counterparts. The German midgets were only used defensively; the British towed theirs behind larger submarines to enable them to reach their targets (thereby losing several in passage). Only the Japanese also carried their midgets to their targets on other submarines.

Below: The submarine Luciano Manara, *seen after her surrender at Malta in September 1943. Bottom: The incomplete aircraft carrier* Aquila *rusting in Genoa – a belated attempt to provide air cover to the Italian fleet. She never saw action because the armistice intervened before her launch*

Capital Ships

In the early 1930s, the only battleships that the Italians possessed were four old, slow, lightly armed and lightly armoured vessels which, though possibly a match for their French equivalents, were certainly no use against the new *Dunkerque* class. They were therefore reconstructed, emerging as completely different vessels. In order to raise the speed by seven knots the hull was lengthened by more than 9 metres by fitting a new bow section. The centre turret was removed to make room for entirely new machinery and boilers of three times the power, driving two instead of four screws. A new superstructure was fitted and the armament was remodelled. The heavy guns were bored out from 305 mm to 320 mm and a new secondary anti-aircraft battery was fitted. The new Pugliese system of underwater protection was introduced and the horizontal armour was strengthened, but it was still inadequate, and nothing could be done about the thin side armour.

The first pair, the *Conte Di Cavour* and *Giulio Cesare*, were converted between 1933 and 1937. The second pair, *Andrea Doria* and *Caio Duilio*, converted between 1937 and 1940, were fitted with a modified secondary armament and a much improved anti-aircraft battery. Their appearance had changed dramatically, for when completed in the First World War they had widely spaced tall funnels and very tall tripod masts like contemporary British dreadnoughts. The midships triple 305-mm gun turret had divided the superstructure into two separate sections, in the same manner as the first Italian dreadnought *Dante Alighieri*. Now all four ships had a forecastle deck which extended for two-thirds of the length, and in place of the midships turret were two smaller funnels with clinker-screens. The tripod masts and small bridge gave way to a prominent bridge with a control tower above it. The anti-aircraft guns were sited on the forecastle deck and the old broadside battery was completely suppressed. The first pair of vessels could be easily distinguished from the second because the later ships had their anti-aircraft guns in single turrets, closely arranged.

Wartime alterations were mostly minor, for the Italian Navy did not have sufficient battle experience to know how many changes were needed. Radar aerials were fitted late in the war and the three survivors were painted in a series of camouflage schemes. Numerous light anti-aircraft guns were added on 'B' turret, the quarter-deck and the superstructure to cope with increased air attacks. The *Conte Di Cavour* never completed her rebuilding and repairs after Taranto, so in December 1941 she went to sea with a new camouflage scheme and extra anti-aircraft guns, but no big guns in her turrets as she was merely in transit from Taranto to Trieste where she would be out of reach of British bombers. The two *Caio Duilio* ships, being completed later, had a more elaborate control tower and more light anti-aircraft guns.

As in the Royal Navy, the Italians drew on the expertise of marine artists in designing camouflage schemes. In the autumn of 1941 the *Andrea Doria* was painted in a four-colour scheme devised by an artist named Claudius; it was a disruptive pattern of saw-toothed black areas over the central part of the superstructure and hull, with panels of dark and light grey and light blue. But the most spectacular design of all was the 'dorsal fin' camouflage scheme worn by the *Duilio* in 1941, with enormous light green arrowheads pointing inwards from both ends of the ship against a dark grey background. The *Giulio Cesare* and *Cavour* both used schemes designed by Claudius in 1941 and 1942, but in 1942–43 the *Cesare*, *Duilio* and *Doria* changed to lighter-coloured patterns. In the post-war Italian Navy the *Duilio* and *Doria* adopted a scheme resembling the Royal Navy's post-war colours, a dark grey hull and light grey upperworks.

Although the conversions were a very successful technical achievement it is doubtful whether the results justified the time and money involved. It is true that Italy needed numbers as well as quality to counteract the five old French battleships, and Washington Naval Treaty tonnage restrictions would have caused problems if new battleships had been laid down without scrapping the old. However, the *Cavour* and the *Duilio* vessels, as reconstructed, were far too weakly protected to stand up even to the old British 15-inch (380-mm) battleships. Also, the underwater protection was inadequate, as was shown at Taranto, when *Cavour* sank and *Duilio* was badly damaged.

Giulio Cesare, *Caio Duilio*, and *Doria* survived the war, and were among the last battleships in service, *Cesare* in the Soviet and *Duilio* and *Doria* in the Italian Navy. The latter two were not finally taken out of service till 1956, about the time that the ex-*Giulio Cesare* was mined and sunk by the Soviet Navy. Though *Cavour* was raised, she was never returned to service and was eventually sunk by an American air raid in 1945.

The problem with battleships was that they represented too big an investment in capital to be discarded. The Italian conversions were not as extreme as the Japanese but they still demonstrate the folly of putting new wine into old bottles. But it must be remembered that the political climate of the 1920s and 1930s, both inside and outside Italy, favoured disarmament. It was therefore inconceivable that the major powers would have agreed to any relaxation of the treaties to allow navies to start building battleships. The whole series of reconstructions in the 1930s must be looked on as attempts to modernize fleets in spite of a hostile climate, and in that light they were justifiable. But in the case of the *Conte di Cavour* and her sisters the original design was poor, and so any amount of reconstruction was unlikely to produce a front-rank battleship capable of facing foreign ships. The obsession with speed did nothing to help the designers. There is no doubt that a more modest speed would have allowed for at least some extra deck armour.

CONTE DI CAVOUR
Displacement 26,140 tons (26,559 tonnes) normal, 29,032 tons (29,498 tonnes) full load
Length 611 feet 6 inches (186 m 38 cm)
Beam 54 feet 4 inches (16 m 55 cm)
Draught 30 feet (9 m 14 cm)
Machinery 2-shaft geared steam turbines, 75,000 shp = 26 knots
Armour belt: 9¾ inches (245 mm). decks: 3⅖ inches (87 mm). turrets: 11 inch (280 mm)
Guns 10 × 12.6-inch (320-mm), 12 × 4.7-inch (120-mm), 8 × 3.9-inch (100-mm) AA, 8 × 37-mm AA, 12 × 20-mm AA
Aircraft none
Launched 10 August 1911 by La Spezia Dockyard

Conte Di Cavour

The *Littorio* class were much more impressive ships. The first two, *Littorio* (renamed *Italia* in 1943) and *Vittorio Veneto*, were laid down in 1934 and the second group, *Impero* and *Roma*, in 1938. Because their designers ignored the 35,500-tonne treaty limitation it is not surprising that these were powerful ships, although the extra 2,000 or more tonnes did not give them as much advantage over their British and American contemporaries as might have been expected. The second group differed from the first mainly by having a different bow to improve the seaworthiness.

These ships were well armed and armoured, with an unusually high command for the after 380-mm turret. Their weakest point, apart from the short range usual in Mediterranean vessels, was their underwater protection. As in the *Cavour* and *Duilio* classes, the Pugliese system was employed, which utilized an empty cylinder to absorb the shock of a torpedo's explosion. This did not work as well in practice as the various systems used by other countries, since the compartmentation was not fully watertight. The first pair of ships were completed just before Italy entered the war, and these fast modern vessels might have had a considerable effect on the war in the Mediterranean if they had been used more adventurously. *Impero* was never completed, and *Roma*, finished near the end of 1943, saw no active service apart from gaining the unfortunate distinction of being the only battleship to be sunk by a guided missile. She

was sunk by a German 1400 X glider bomb on her way to surrender at Malta in September 1943, and *Italia* (ex-*Littorio*) was damaged by a hit and a near miss on the same occasion. It is interesting to note that there were proposals to use *Vittorio Veneto* and *Italia* to reinforce the British Far Eastern Fleet near the end of the war, but their short range and anticipated problems with equipment and spares prevented this.

In appearance the *Littorio* vessels differed widely from the older ships, although the compact control tower and small capped funnels stamped them as coming out of the same stable. The most obvious recognition point was the after 380-mm triple gun turret, which was on the same level as 'B' turret, and the aircraft catapult on the quarterdeck. Apart from the addition of 20-mm anti-aircraft guns on the superstructure and on the 152-mm gun turrets, and radar aerials on the control tower, little was done to alter the *Littorio* vessels between 1940 and 1943.

In the spring of 1941 the *Littorio* was painted in a 'fish-tail' camouflage scheme, but using a very dark grey background. Her sister *Vittorio Veneto* adopted the same scheme but used the lighter grey that was tried in the *Duilio*. In 1943 there was more variation, with the *Littorio* (now renamed *Italia* in an effort to purge memories of Fascism) painted in two tones of grey, with dark irregular patterns, whereas the *Vittorio Veneto* had a series of dark triangular patterns. On her last voyage the luckless *Roma*

was painted with rhomboidal patches all over her hull and superstructure.

The *Littorio* class were unusual in carrying not only floatplanes for reconnaissance but a fighter to shoot down enemy reconnaissance planes. The floatplane was the 311 km/h IMAM Ro 43 biplane, and the fighter was the 531 km/h Reggiane 2000 Falco Serie II monoplane. The idea was sound, and resembled the policy of the Japanese, who developed a floatplane fighter for similar purposes, but in the Mediterranean the Italian shipboard aircraft were far more likely to run into carrier-based fighters than the lumbering Walruses and Seafoxes that the Falco fighter was supposed to defeat. No protection was given to the aircraft on the catapult, either from the sea or from the blast of the 380-mm turret, and there are many photographs to show how badly the aircraft suffered.

The two survivors, the *Italia* and *Vittorio Veneto*, sailed for Malta after the surrender and were laid up in the Bitter Lakes on the Suez Canal. Their disposal was complicated by the fact that Italy was now a gallant Ally. After the abortive discussions about 'tropicalizing' them to act as fast carrier escorts in the Far East, it was reluctantly agreed among the Allies that it would be better to scrap them. This was almost certainly dictated by a desire to prevent one of them from falling into Soviet hands, as the Soviets staked their claim to a fair share of Italian tonnage by way of reparations. Instead, the Soviets were given the *Giulio Cesare*, while

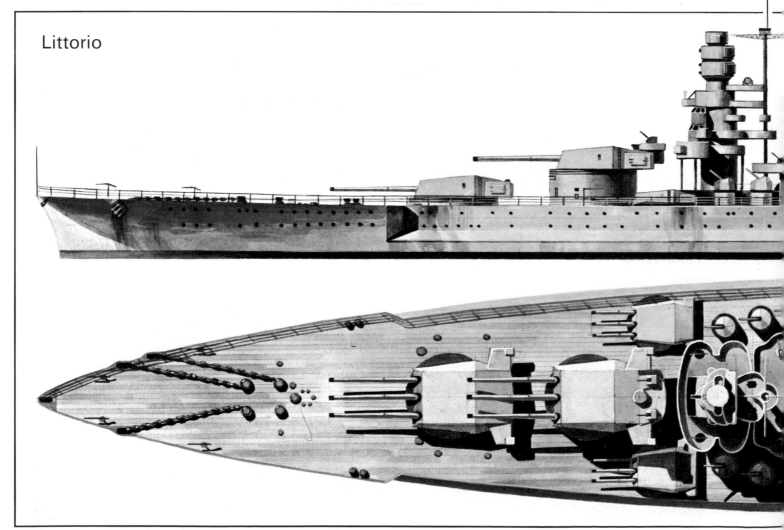

Littorio

the elegant but ineffective *Littorio* vessels went to the breakers' yards. By 1951 the demolition work was completed at La Spezia.

The *Littorio* class were among the best-looking warships of the Second World War, and although by no means the best battleships of their day they could well have given a good account in action. Their secondary armament was too crowded for efficiency, with the triple 152-mm turrets crowding the anti-aircraft turrets into a serried rank on the broadside where they had restricted arcs of fire. Looking back, they had restricted arcs of fire.

LITTORIO

Displacement 41,377 tons (42,041 tonnes) normal, 45,963 tons (46,700 tonnes) full load
Length 780 feet 8 inches (237 m 94 cm)
Beam 108 feet (32 m 91 cm)
Draught 31 feet 5 inches (9 m 56.5 cm)
Machinery 4-shaft geared steam turbines, 130,000 shp = 28 knots
Armour belt: 13¾ inches (348 mm). deck: 3.9 to 8.1 inches (100 to 204 mm). turrets: 13¾ inches (348 mm)
Guns 9 × 15-inch (380-mm), 12 × 6-inch (152-mm), 12 × 3.5-inch (88 mm) AA, 4 × 4.7-inch (120-mm) (for starshell), 20 × 37-mm AA, 28 × 20-mm AA
Aircraft 3 (1 catapult)
Launched 22 August 1937 by Ansaldo, Genoa

The Littorio *in her 1943 camouflage scheme with two RO43 biplane reconnaisance aircraft. The illustration shows a Reggiane 2000 monoplane fighter on the catapult*

Cruisers

As with the French, the early Italian interwar light and heavy cruisers were fast but had short range and very little armour. Some of the early 'Condottieri'-type light cruisers achieved very high trial speeds because the Italians habitually ran their speed trial with the ships very lightly loaded, sometimes even before the armament had been mounted. As a result, the maximum speeds that Italian warships attained in service were often no greater than those of their apparently slower British opponents, whose trial speeds had been obtained at normal service displacements. It was realized that the *Trento*-class heavy cruisers in particular were far too lightly armoured, and the succeeding *Zara* class were given much heavier armour. Laid down between 1929 and 1931, these four vessels had a well-balanced design, a condition made more easy to achieve by ignoring the Washington Naval Treaty. Instead of a maximum standard displacement of 10,160 tonnes, the actual designed standard displacement of the *Zara* vessels was nearly 12,190 tonnes. It was no reflection on the fighting qualities of the ships themselves that three of the class, *Zara*, *Pola* and *Fiume*, were sunk at Matapan; even heavy cruisers are not expected to withstand the fire of 15-inch-(380-mm)-gunned battleships at 4,000 yards (3.7 km).

The *Zara* and *Fiume* were built under the 1928–29 programme. the *Gorizia* in the following year's programme, and the *Pola* a year later. The first ship completed was the *Zara* in 1931 and her tests indicate how misleading trials data can be. During her eight-hour trial without guns or turrets, the ship reached a maximum speed of 34.2 knots with nearly 118,000 shaft horsepower. Unfortunately her displacement was already 10,970 tonnes and once she received her armament the displacement jumped to 13,800 tonnes. As a result her 'sea speed', the speed which she could make at sea when normally loaded with fuel and ammunition, was 29 knots, not enough to keep her out of trouble if caught by foreign cruisers.

The only one of the class to be camouflaged in 1940–41 was the *Fiume*. She had an experimental disruptive scheme painted in March 1941, only a few weeks before her loss at Matapan, but as only one poor photograph of her was taken it is impossible to know the details of it. The others retained the attractive light grey, almost off-white hull and upperworks with black funnel caps which made Italian cruisers look so impressive. Diagonal red and white stripes were painted on the forecastle for recognition by aircraft, but it does not appear to have been effective; the *Regia Aeronautica* often bombed Italian ships by mistake.

The Italians were the only navy to put aircraft on the forecastle. The *Zara* class carried a catapult and two IMAM Ro 43 floatplanes (replacing older models of aircraft fitted before the war). Unlike the battleships' aircraft these

Left: Italian 203-mm gunned cruisers at sea.
Right: The cruiser Gorizia *was the only one of her class to survive the Battle of Matapan. She is seen here at Kiel in 1936, with a German 'pocket battleship' in the background*

were provided with a hangar underneath the forecastle. From here the floatplanes were lifted out by a derrick which was normally stowed. The position was exposed to gun-blast and spray; interference was encountered if the ship steamed into a head sea, and the hangar was awkwardly placed.

The *Pola* was the unwitting cause of the disaster in which she and her two sisters met their end at the Battle of Cape Matapan. She was one of the ships screening the damaged *Vittorio Veneto* on the evening of 27 March 1941, but just as darkness was closing in a British carrier aircraft hit her with a single torpedo. The battleship was able to slip away at 19 knots but the *Pola* was soon unable to steam, and the 1st Cruiser Division was ordered to assist her. The *Fiume* was just getting ready to take the *Pola* in tow when a single searchlight lit up the *Zara*, followed immediately by broadsides of 15-inch (380-mm) shells from the British battleships *Valiant* and *Warspite*. More searchlights and starshells followed and in quick succession the other two cruisers came under a withering fire. The *Pola* was the last to sink, and British destroyers came alongside to take off 258 survivors before torpedoing her.

The sole survivor of the class, the *Gorizia*, was finally sunk at La Spezia by Italian frogmen operating under British control. She had been taken over by the Germans at the time of the Italian surrender in September 1943.

POLA
Displacement 11,500 tons (11,684 tonnes) normal, 14,200 tons (14,427 tonnes) full load
Length 599 feet 9 inches (182 m 80 cm)
Beam 67 feet 7 inches (20 m 59.5 cm)
Draught 19 feet 4 inches (5 m 18 cm)
Machinery 2-shaft geared steam turbines, 95,000 shp = 29 knots
Armour belt: 5.9 inches (152 mm). deck: $2\frac{3}{4}$ inches (70 mm). turrets: 5.9 inches (152 mm)
Guns 8 × 8-inch (203-mm), 12 × 3.9-inch (100-mm) AA, 8 × 37-mm AA
Aircraft 2 (1 catapult)
Launched 5 December 1931 by Odero-Terni-Orlando, Livorno

Pola, unlike Gorizia, *had the bridge structure streamlined into the forefunnel*

Pola

The light cruisers were developed in a much more gradual fashion. The first class, which included *Giovanni Delle Bande Nere*, were laid down in 1928, and the last of the five classes, the *Giuseppe Garibaldi* and the ship with perhaps the longest name of any in the Second World War, *Luigi Di Savoia Duca Degli Abruzzi*, were completed in 1937. Each class were somewhat larger than their predecessors, had thicker armour, and were slightly slower. The last class also had two more 152-mm and two more 100-mm guns than the others. Thus *Giovanni Delle Bande Nere* had a displacement of 5,280 tonnes, a designed speed of 37 knots, an armament of eight 152-mm and six 100-mm guns and 25-mm side armour, whereas the *Giuseppe Garibaldi*, on a displacement of 9,537 tonnes, had a designed speed of 35 knots (which it did not reach), an armament of ten 152-mm and eight 100-mm guns, and 145-mm side armour.

Except for the *Garibaldi* class, these light cruisers were not very good designs, too much emphasis having been placed on speed. As a result they were very lightly built, with too small an amount of the displacement being devoted to protection.

Also classed as light cruisers, but equivalent to and only slightly larger than the French large destroyers *Mogador* and *Volta*, were the 12 vessels of the 'Capitani Romani' class. Laid down in 1939 and 1940, only three were completed during the war. The main armament was eight 135-mm guns, and the designed speed was 41 knots. These were a direct reply to the continued French construction of their *Contre Torpilleurs*.

The *Giovanni Delle Bande Nere* and her class represent the extreme of Italian cruiser design, with thin armour and ultra-high speed. The 1939 edition of *Jane's Fighting Ships* claimed that the *Alberto Di Giussano* had reached 42.04 knots on trials and had maintained 39.74 knots for eight hours with full armament aboard. The only point in dispute is whether the armament was on board, as the sea speed of the class was only 30 knots. This helps to explain why the *Bartolomeo Colleoni* and the *Giovanni Delle Bande Nere* were caught in July 1940.

The aircraft arrangement was similar to that of the *Zara* class, with two floatplanes launched from a catapult on the forecastle. But in the light cruisers the aircraft hangar was in the forward superstructure, with steel roller shutters to port and starboard.

The most unusual feature of the design was the machinery. With only two shafts they had a designed horsepower of 95,000, which was exceeded by nearly 30 per cent. The engine-rooms and boiler-rooms took up nearly half the length of the ship, because the turbines and boilers were staggered. The after boiler-room had two Yarrow-Ansaldo boilers, but the forward one contained four boilers, and the distance between them accounted for the widely spaced funnels which became typical of Italian cruisers.

As a class they were unlucky. The *Bartolomeo Colleoni* was caught off Crete by the *Sydney* in July 1940, but on that occasion the *Giovanni Delle Bande Nere* escaped. In December 1941 the *Alberico Da Barbiano* and *Alberto Di Giussano* were loaded with highly inflammable fuel in a desperate attempt to replenish Italian Army stocks in North Africa, but they were caught and sunk by a force of British and Dutch destroyers. The *Giovanni Delle Bande Nere* lasted until April 1942, and was then torpedoed by a British submarine a month after being in action against British cruisers at the Battle of Sirte.

GIOVANNI DELLE BANDE NERE
Displacement 5,200 tons (5,283 tonnes) normal, 7,000 tons (7,112 tonnes) full load
Length 555 feet 5 inches (169 m 30 cm)
Beam 50 feet 10 inches (15 m 48 cm)
Draught 16 feet 1 inches (4 m 89 cm)
Machinery 2-shaft geared steam turbines, 95,000 shp = 30 knots
Armour belt: 1 inch (25 mm). deck: $\frac{7}{8}$ inch (21 mm). turrets: 1 inch (25 mm)
Guns 8 × 6-inch (152-mm), 6 × 3.9-inch (100-mm) AA, 8 × 37-mm AA
Torpedo Tubes 4 × 21-inch (532-mm)
Aircraft 2 (1 catapult)
Launched 27 April 1930 by Castellamare di Stabia Dockyard

The fast but fragile Italian light cruiser Bande Nere. *The forward uptake is trunked back to take funnel gas well clear of the bridge*

Giovanni Delle Bande Nere

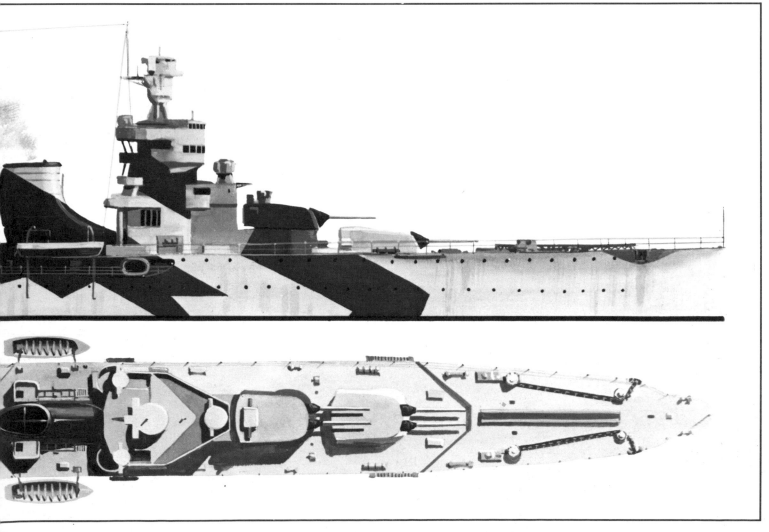

JAPAN

In relation to the tasks it had to perform the Japanese Navy had more problems than any other, both before and during the Second World War. Of all the combatants, only Britain and Japan were immediately dependent on seaborne trade. However, Britain not only possessed a large navy and shipbuilding industry but also acquired most of her raw materials from countries either directly controlled by her or at least friendly. In addition, her most likely opponents had smaller navies. Japan, on the other hand, had a navy fixed by the Washington Treaty at only three-fifths the size of the navies of Britain and her most likely opponent throughout the interwar period, the United States. The Japanese shipbuilding industry was small and the industrial base on which it depended was limited, so there was no possibility of expansion. In any case (despite persistent rumours – taken seriously by many Japanese planners – of America's inability to cope with a war situation due to lack of nerve) there was never the remotest possibility of Japan equalling America's *potential* war production. When war came, America was able simultaneously to repair all the salvable ships from Pearl Harbor and build an enormous war programme, a feat that Japan could never hope to emulate. Also, almost all Japan's supplies of raw materials were controlled by Britain,

Holland and the United States. These three countries held a stranglehold on the most vital of all materials, oil.

Yet it was essential that the Japanese Navy should be strong enough to ensure control of home waters and have at least a chance of defeating the American Navy. It also needed to control enough of the Pacific to guarantee sufficient raw materials; to win a war, Japan would have to expand.

This ruled out one possible solution, large numbers of relatively cheap small ships. To take the offensive, quality as well as quantity was necessary. In addition the vast distances of the Pacific necessitated relatively large ships, carrying sufficient fuel to ensure adequate range. By the 1930s the Japanese naval high command was split into two competing groups. The larger

group favoured the traditional idea of luring the American battlefleet into Japanese home waters and defeating the numerically superior American battleships with a smaller number of individually superior Japanese ones. The other group favoured a more aggressive policy based on a large striking force of fast aircraft carriers. Because of Japan's limited shipbuilding capability it was not possible to satisfy both requirements, but this is just what she disastrously attempted to do, tying up a large percentage of the shipbuilding industry by constructing an insufficient number of large battleships, while at the same time being unable to build an overwhelming carrier force. Partly because of the need to win quickly, neither faction gave much thought to the provision of anti-submarine escorts for the merchant fleet. This was to

render much quicker and easier the American submarines' destruction of the Japanese economy when war did break out.

It used to be said that the Japanese were mere copiers. While it is true that they made good use of other countries' designs, they were also great innovators. They were the first to successfully employ turrets on destroyers, and also the first to equip destroyers with dual-purpose guns. The 'Long Lance' torpedo was far and away the best in the world, and the Japanese helped to ensure its success by fitting the later destroyer classes with efficient reloading systems. If their submarines took a long time to dive in an emergency, and were noisy by contemporary standards, they were also impressive technical achievements.

Where the Japanese designers went astray was in their persistent efforts to get around treaty tonnage restrictions by putting too heavy an armament on too small a hull which they attempted to drive at too fast a speed. This resulted in ships whose hulls were too lightly built to cope even with the sea, let alone with battle damage, and whose instability was such that many Japanese warships built in the 1930s were in imminent danger of capsizing. By the time these ships had been strengthened, rebuilt and reballasted they displaced as much as their foreign contemporaries, which, however, had the advantage of being designed to make use of the larger displacement. The Japanese were much more successful when they evaded the treaty by lying about the tonnage and building their ships bigger.

The urge to build ships individually more powerful than any possible opponent was quite an understandable one. As has been explained earlier, not only could the Japanese not hope to outbuild America in an emergency, but the terms of the Washington Treaty kept her numerically inferior. While the Japanese did not use their resources to the utmost advantage (indeed, some of the decisions of the naval staff and their designers were completely indefensible), it is difficult to see what Japan could have done to give her a reasonable chance of victory.

It was a grave error not to build *any* specialized anti-submarine escort vessels until 1940, and very few were built after that. Escort carriers should and could have been provided early in the war. However, in a situation where not to attack was to lose, the lack of emphasis on defence measures is understandable if inexcusable.

All Japan could hope for was a stalemate, and even the possibility of this was denied her by the poor quality of her high command. One is left in the end, however, with a good deal of sympathy for the Japanese because of the impossible nature of the problem they faced.

The Japanese had a great deal of experience with carriers. Their first, *Hosho*, though laid down after HMS *Hermes*, was completed sooner, and was thus the first purpose-designed carrier to be built. Small and slow, she was taken off active duty after the Battle of Midway and used for training. However, the next two carriers, the *Akagi* and the *Kaga*, were much more valuable ships.

The giant Japanese battleship Yamato *undergoes trials in heavy weather in December 1941. The uneven deckline is faintly discernible through the spray, and the hanger opening right aft. Note the massive rangefinder on the control tower, the sharply raked and trunked funnel and the triple 155-mm gun turrets*

Aircraft Carriers

Under the provision of the Washington Treaty it had been intended that the incomplete battle-cruisers *Amagi* and *Akagi* should not be scrapped as originally proposed, but completed as carriers to match the American *Lexington* and *Saratoga*. Unfortunately the hull of *Amagi* was so badly damaged by an earthquake in 1923 that it had to be scrapped, and the hull of the incomplete *Kaga*, one of the companion class of battleships also due to be scrapped under the Washington Treaty, was used instead. As finally converted, *Kaga* was 12 m 17 cm shorter, 2,000 tonnes heavier and 3 knots slower than *Akagi*, but they carried virtually the same number of aircraft, and usually operated together. Indeed, after her 1936–38 refit, *Akagi* was fitted with her bridge on the port side instead of the normal starboard side (as it was on *Kaga*), so that when

they operated together the landing circuits of their aircraft would be in opposite directions. It was hoped that this would avoid accidents and speed the rate of recovery of the aircraft. *Soryu* had her bridge to starboard and her half-sister *Hiryu* had hers to port for the same reason. When these four ships operated together at the Battle of Midway, their formation was arranged to take advantage of this.

However, having the bridge on the port side was not a success. Air turbulence caused problems and increased the rate of landing accidents, so no other carrier had the bridge to port. Both *Kaga* and *Akagi* retained a thick waterline belt, and each was armed initially with ten 203-mm guns and had three flight decks forward.

Originally *Kaga* had two long funnels, one on either side of main flight deck, exhausting astern.

During a major refit from 1934–36 this was replaced with a single funnel angled slightly downwards exhausting amidships. In contrast to the original arrangement this gave little trouble. Bulges were fitted, and the ship was lengthened 8.5 m at the stern. New machinery was fitted, raising the speed slightly. At the same time the 203-mm guns were removed and the main flight deck extended from bow to stern, the subsidiary flight decks being removed. This enabled the hangars to be enlarged, and the number of aircraft carried was increased from 60 to 90. A navigating bridge was erected on the previously flush flight deck. The two existing lifts were enlarged and a third added forward.

Akagi's refit was slightly less extensive. As time and money were at a premium, bulges were fitted but only four 203-mm were landed. Even

Kaga

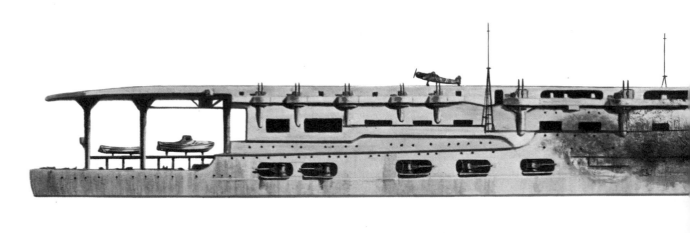

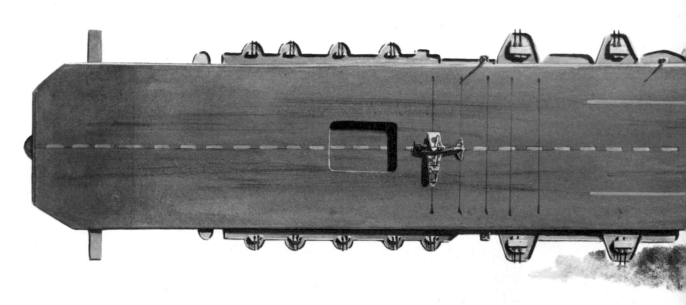

so the main flight deck was extended from bow to stern, and additional hangar space raised the aircraft complement from 60 to 91. The two original lifts were enlarged and a third was added forward, and a navigating bridge erected. All the boilers were converted to oil firing which raised the power slightly. A little smaller and somewhat slower than *Lexington* and *Saratoga*, after their 1930s facelift *Kaga* and *Akagi* compared favourably with them.

Laid down in 1929, the next carrier, *Ryujo*, was completed in 1933. Originally designed to displace about 7,620 tonnes to take advantage of the fact that the Washington Treaty did not limit the number of carriers of less than 10,160 tonnes that each country could build, she was altered while being built to include two hangar decks instead of one. Too much was attempted

on too small a displacement, and she was top-heavy, a fault that many Japanese interwar designs suffered from. The dangers of this were highlighted in March 1934, when the torpedo boat *Tomozuru* capsized in a storm from this cause. Immediately afterwards four of the 127-mm anti-aircraft guns on the *Ryujo* were removed and a ballast keel fitted. Then in September 1935 the Japanese Combined Fleet encountered a storm in the Pacific; almost all the ships were damaged, and two destroyers were lost. After this, the hulls of most Japanese warships were strengthened and topweight was removed. *Ryujo* herself had her forecastle raised by one deck to improve her seaworthiness. All these modifications raised her displacement to 10,776 tonnes, but she would have been a more successful design if that had been her designed tonnage.

KAGA
Displacement 38,200 tons (38,813 tonnes) normal, 43,000 tons (43,690 tonnes) full load
Length 812 feet 4 inches (247 m 59 cm)
Beam 100 feet (30 m 47 cm) over flight deck
Draught 31 feet (9 m 44 cm)
Machinery 4-shaft geared steam turbines, 127,400 shp = 28 knots
Armour belt: 11 inch (280 mm) probably retained. deck: 4 to 6 inches (105 to 152 mm)
Guns 10 × 8-inch (203-mm), 16 × 5-inch (127-mm) DP, 22 × 25-mm AA
Aircraft 72 (2 catapults)
Launched 17 November 1921 by Kawasaki Co., Kobe

The aircraft carrier Kaga shows traces of her battleship origin. Note the 203-mm guns in casemates, the small island superstructure and the downward-curved funnel

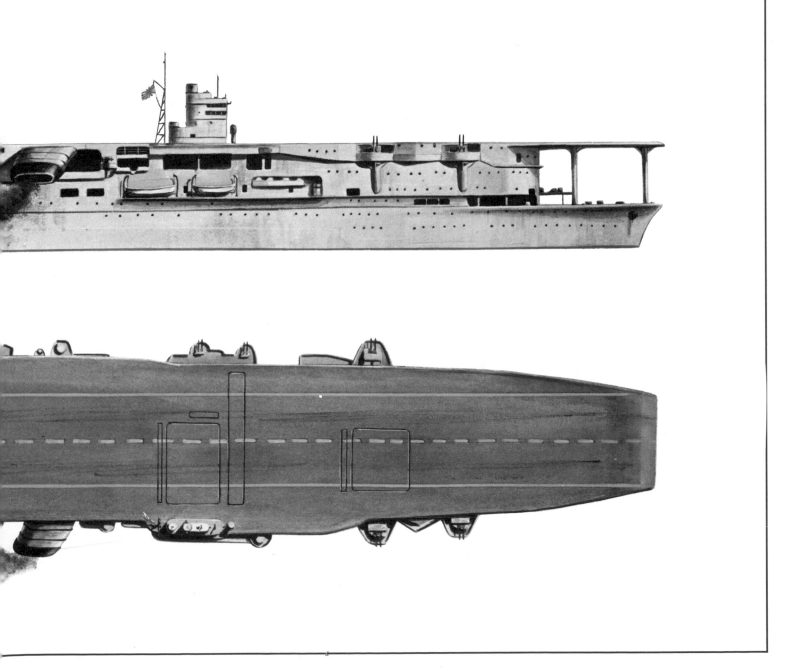

In any case, *Ryujo* was far too small for a fleet carrier. Much more successful was the 16,150-tonne *Soryu*, laid down in 1934; she was only able to be built because Japan had so continuously understated her carrier tonnage that there appeared to be enough left under the terms of the Washington Treaty to build another one which was not in fact the case. Nevertheless, *Soryu* was built, and she formed the basis of the design of most subsequent Japanese Navy carriers. With a speed of more than 34 knots and able to carry over 50 aircraft, she was a formidable vessel.

Her half-sister *Hiryu* was very similar but was built after the expiry of the terms of the Washington Treaty, so the tonnage limitations no longer applied. Thus she was able to take advantage of the lessons of the great storm in 1935, and was modified to improve her seaworthiness. She had 900 mm more beam, her forecastle was one deck higher, her hull was stronger and her displacement was nearly 1,525 tonnes greater. Even so she was smaller and could carry fewer aircraft than her American contemporaries of the *Yorktown* class. As previously noted, *Hiryu* shared with *Akagi* the dubious distinction of being the only carriers with a bridge to port of the flight deck.

Although *Hiryu* was built after the end of the treaty restrictions her size had been governed by that of *Soryu*. The next pair of fleet carriers, *Shokaku* and *Zuikaku*, were the first Japanese carriers since *Hosho* whose design was governed solely by operational requirements.

Basically enlarged and improved versions of the *Hiryu*, they each displaced over 25,400 tonnes and could operate over 80 planes. Utilizing the same sort of bulbous bow as the contemporary *Yamato*, they had a maximum speed of more than 34 knots and an extended range. The 160,000 shaft horsepower developed by their engines was the largest of any Japanese warship. In addition, they possessed the heavy (for 1941) anti-aircraft armament of sixteen 127-mm and thirty-six 25-mm anti-aircraft guns. Each had three lifts (*Soryu* had only two), and after the unhappy experiences with *Akagi* and *Hiryu*, both had their bridges on the starboard side of the flight deck. When they were completed a few months before Pearl Harbor they were the most powerful carriers in the Pacific. Well-balanced designs, they were the most successful of all the Japanese carriers, and their enforced absence from the Midway operation due to battle damage and lack of trained pilots was a misfortune for the Japanese.

However, in one respect neither they nor any other Japanese or American carriers of the late 1930s measured up to their British contemporaries. The first shortfall was the lack of an armoured flight deck, which was by deliberate choice. Royal Navy carriers would be forced to operate for much of the time within range of shore-based aircraft which would be available in numbers sufficient to swamp any fighter defence the carriers could put up. Therefore the defence of the British carrier rested ultimately on its own anti-aircraft armament and as much horizontal armour as possible. Because armoured flight decks put a lot of weight high up in a ship, the hangars had to be small to avoid top-heaviness. Therefore the number of planes carried was small. In the Pacific the problems were different. Distances were too great for land-based aircraft to be considered the prime threat. The greatest need was for a large aircraft-carrying capacity to provide overwhelming strike force as well as sufficient fighters for escort and carrier defence. Therefore armoured flight decks were not fitted.

Wartime experience showed that this was the wrong decision. Whereas British carriers with armoured flight decks survived to be repaired, and frequently were able to continue operating

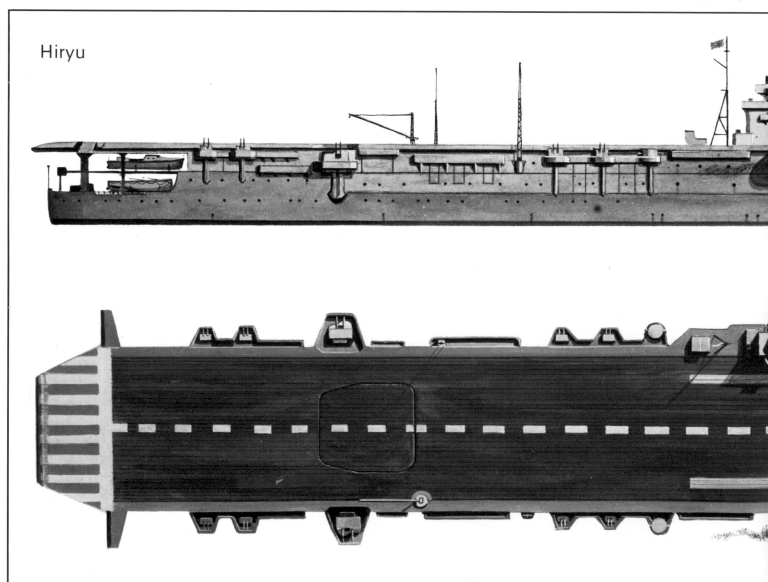

Hiryu

aircraft even after quite large bomb hits, the unarmoured flight decks of their Japanese and American contemporaries were easily put out of action by even minor damage, and the carriers themselves were much more easily sunk by air attack. Although *Shokaku* survived two battles (Coral Sea and Santa Cruz) at which her flight deck was so badly damaged as to render her incapable of operating aircraft, such resistance to battle damage was rare among Japanese carriers.

HIRYU
Displacement 17,300 tons (17,577 tonnes) normal, 21,000 tons (21,337 tonnes) full load
Length 746 feet (227 m 38 cm)
Beam 88 feet 6 inches (26 m 97 cm) over flight deck
Draught 25 feet 4 inches (7 m 72 cm)
Machinery 4-shaft geared steam turbines, 152,000 shp = 34½ knots
Armour unknown, but probably a waterline belt and deck protection
Guns 12 × 5-inch (127-mm) DP, 31 × 25-mm AA
Aircraft 73 (2 catapults)
Launched 16 November 1937 by Yokosuka Dockyard

Hiryu on trials in April 1939; note the distinctive port-side island

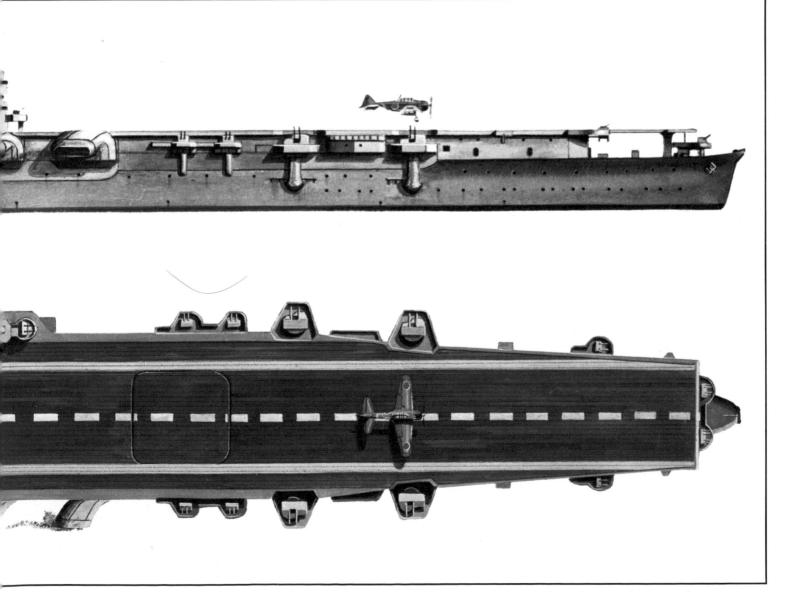

Shoho

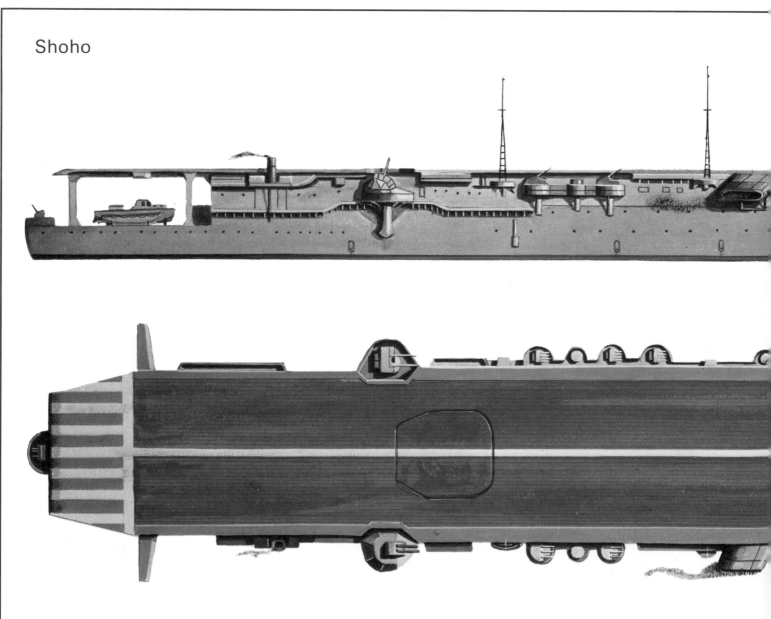

Realizing that there would be neither time nor shipbuilding capacity available if Japan became involved in a major war, the naval high command had arranged that a number of fleet auxiliaries and large liners should be designed in such a way that they could swiftly and easily be converted into light carriers if the need arose, and in 1940 the first steps were taken to convert them. The *Shoho* and *Zuiho* (ex-*Tsurugizaki* and *Takasaki* respectively) had been laid down in 1934 as high-speed oilers, but it was later decided that they should be completed as submarine tenders. *Tsurugizaki* was actually completed in this form in 1938 and her conversion into a carrier did not start till early 1941. *Takasaki* was still under construction when in January 1940 it was decided to complete her as a carrier. These ships were originally fitted with

Shoho was built as the submarine depot ship Tsurugizaki. She was not renamed until December 1941, two days after this photograph was taken. Note the raised barrier on the flight deck and the hinged radio masts which would be lowered during flying operations

diesels because the potential advantages of this type of engine – lower fuel consumption and less weight – were what were needed to provide the ships with greater range while at the same time releasing a greater proportion of the displacement for armament and protection. Like the Germans, the Japanese made extensive experiments with diesels in the interwar period, but the Japanese never managed to get their diesels to perform with sufficient reliability for active service. For this reason *Shoho* and *Zuiho* were fitted with turbines when they were converted into carriers. No armour was fitted because this would have reduced the ships' performance, which was already very low for vessels intended to act with the fleet. The slightly larger *Ryuho* (ex-*Taigei*), laid down in 1931 as a submarine tender, was converted in the same way as *Shoho* and *Zuiho*. Designed and built in a hurry, the extensive electrical welding used to speed her construction gave trouble, as did her extremely unreliable diesels which were replaced with turbines during reconstruction. Partly because of this the conversion, planned to take three months, in fact took 12. Completed in late 1942,

she was never used operationally and was one of the four Japanese carriers that survived the war.

Designed to be convertible into high-speed oilers, submarine tenders, seaplane carriers or aircraft carriers, *Chiyoda* and *Chitose* were completed in 1938 as high-speed seaplane tenders, with four catapults apiece and a mix of diesel and steam turbine engines that they retained for the rest of their career. With the loss of four large carriers at Midway, Japan's need for carriers became pressing, and conversion of both *Chitose* and *Chiyoda* was begun in late 1942 and early

SHOHO
Displacement 11,262 tons (11,442 tonnes) normal, 15,000 tons (15,240 tonnes) full load
Length 712 feet (217 m)
Beam 75 feet 6 inches (23 m) over flight deck
Draught 21 feet 9 inches (6 m 62 cm)
Machinery 2-shaft geared steam turbines, 52,000 shp = 28 knots
Armour none
Guns 8 × 5-inch (127-mm) DP, 8 × 25-mm AA
Aircraft 30 (2 catapults)
Launched 1 June 1935 (as *Tsurugizaki*) by Yokosuka Dockyard

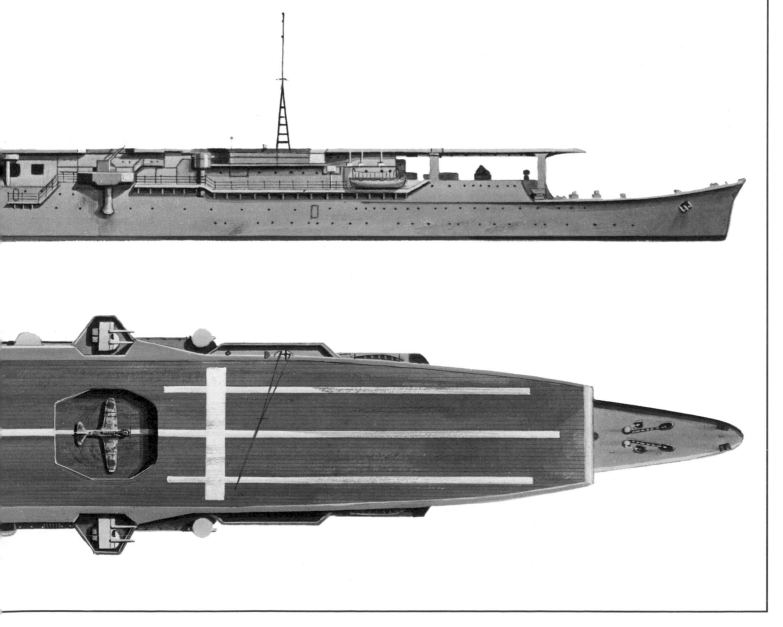

1943. As converted they resembled the *Shoho* class closely, except for their mixed propulsion.

Taiyo, *Chuyo* and *Unyo* (ex-*Kasuga Maru*, *Nitta Maru* and *Yawata Maru* respectively) were converted into carriers. *Taiyo* was converted in 1941 and *Unyo* from January to May 1942, but the conversion of *Chuyu* was delayed because she was intended to carry a Japanese delegation to a proposed conference with President Roosevelt in late 1941. In the event, her conversion was not completed until November 1942. Because they lacked catapults and arrestor gear, these ships were not suitable for service with the fleet, while for escort and training duties they were unnecessarily large and fast. They were mostly used as aircraft ferries and training carriers, and their large size merely served to provide a large target for the submarines that eventually sunk all three. Considerably better fitted for fleet work were the *Hiyo* and *Junyo*. Converted in an early stage of construction, these ships (originally intended as the luxury liners *Izumo Maru* and *Kashiwara Maru* respectively) were over 6,000 tonnes larger and nearly five knots faster than the *Taiyo* class. Most nearly comparable with the British light fleet carriers, these were the first carriers in the Japanese Navy to have both the bridge and funnel mounted above the flight deck, and were valuable additions to the fleet.

Also converted from liners were *Kaiyo* and *Shinyo*. *Kaiyo* (ex-*Argentina Maru*) was completed as a liner in 1939 and her conversion was finished in late 1943. She was the smallest liner the Japanese converted, and in an effort to increase her speed they replaced her existing engines with a set of destroyer turbines, but even so she could only make 23 knots. This would have been more than adequate for escort work, but the Japanese mistakenly intended to use all these conversions for fleet work, for which purpose she, like the *Taiyo*, was too slow. Like them, she was used for training and as an aircraft ferry. Her sister *Brazil Maru* was sunk as a transport before she could be converted.

Shinyo was a conversion of the German liner *Scharnhorst*, caught in Far Eastern waters by the outbreak of war. She had been the test ship for the new German high-pressure boilers, which proved as unreliable in her as in all the German ships they were used in; they were replaced shortly after conversion. As completed she was similar to the ships of the *Taiyo* class, except that she was fitted with bulges and a radar aerial. Steel for her conversion was taken from the incomplete hull of the forth *Yamato*-class battleship.

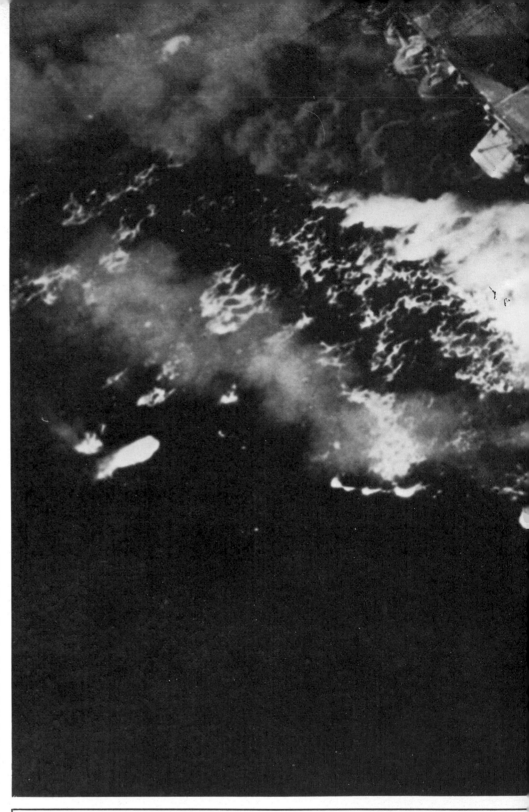

ZUIHO
Displacement 11,262 tons (11,442 tonnes) normal, 15,000 tons (15,240 tonnes) full load
Length 712 feet (217 m)
Beam 75 feet 6 inches (23 m) over flight deck
Draught 21 feet 9 inches (6 m 62 cm)
Machinery 2-shaft geared steam turbines, 52,000 shp = 28 knots
Armour none
Guns 8 × 5-inch (127-mm) DP, 8 × 25-mm AA
Aircraft 30 (2 catapults)
Launched 19 June 1936 (as *Takasaki*) by Yokosuka Dockyard

The carrier Zuiho, *a sister of the* Shoho, *seen shortly before she sank during the Battle of Leyte Gulf. The camouflage scheme tried to give the impression of a battleship*

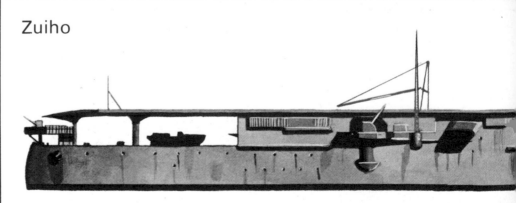

Zuiho

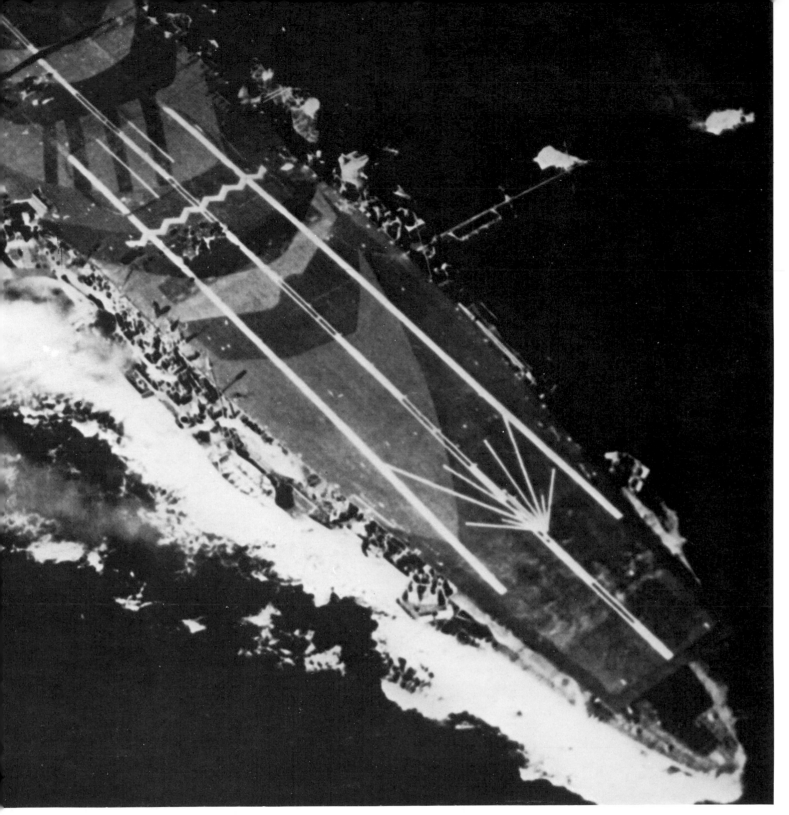

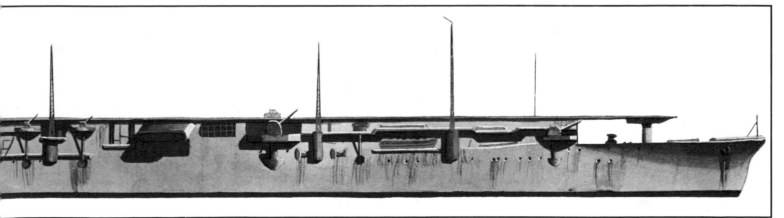

Taiho, laid down in 1941 but not completed until 1944, was the first Japanese fleet carrier to be completed that incorporated the results of combat experience from the war in the Atlantic and in the Mediterranean and from Japan's own experience in the Pacific. Much the same size as *Shokaku*, she had one deck less owing to having an armoured deck (though this was only a deck, and not a box as in British carriers) and therefore carried only two-thirds the number of aircraft. She also carried a large anti-aircraft armament and was the first Japanese fleet carrier to have her bridge and funnel above the flight deck. The bow was also plated up to this level, giving superior seaworthiness in heavy seas. While *Taiho* was a competent design, she was not perhaps quite as good as one might expect of a carrier completed so late in the war. Four slightly larger variants were ordered in the two emergency programmes following Midway, and a further three were proposed, but they were all cancelled. *Taiho* was eventually lost after being torpedoed because of poor damage control, to which the badly thought-out fuel storage and distribution arrangements contributed.

Laid down in 1942, *Unryu* was a very slightly altered *Hiryu* with the bridge moved to the starboard side of the flight deck and an augmented anti-aircraft armament. Five more were laid down after Midway, of which only *Amagi* and *Katsuragi* were completed. *Kasagi* was almost finished when work stopped in April 1945, but *Aso* and *Ikoma* had not even been fitted with hangars by the end of the war. Only two lifts were fitted in these ships to simplify construction, and because there were no suitable large engines, *Aso* and *Katsuragi* were fitted with destroyer turbines which reduced the power by thirty per cent and lowered the speed by two knots. Eleven more were ordered, but they were all cancelled before being laid down. Although the *Hiryu* was a reasonable design for the mid-1930s, by 1944 it had become somewhat dated, and the *Unryu* class were too small and too badly protected for their designed function as Pacific fleet carriers in the later part of the war.

Following these vessels came two warship conversions. The first, *Shinano*, was laid down in May 1940 as the third *Yamato*-class battleship. After Midway the design was altered and the virtually complete hull was fitted with an armoured flight deck. As first recast, her design did not envisage her operating any aircraft of her own. Instead she was intended to act as a base for the planes from other carriers, refuelling, repairing and maintaining them at sea. Because of this she was to be fitted with only a small amount of hangar space, but would have large stocks of fuel, bombs, torpedoes and spare parts stored in the spaces where her turrets were to have been. In time it was recognized that she would need some planes of her own for self-protection, and so provision was made for her to operate some, but she never had the chance to use them in action for she was torpedoed and sunk on her maiden voyage. Hit by four torpedoes aft, from the American submarine *Archerfish*, she proceeded at 16 knots for her destination; *Shinano* still had her battleship protection, and it was thought that she would be able to survive. However, her crew were untrained, and production standards as well as the quality of materials had deteriorated during the war. As a result, many compartments that ought to have been watertight were not, and some watertight doors were missing. At 16 knots water poured into the hull, and she sank after a few hours.

The other warship conversion, *Ibuki*, had been laid down in 1942 as a heavy cruiser. Owing to the pressing shortage of tankers, it was at first decided to complete her as a high-speed oiler, but this was never put into effect. In late 1943 it was decided to convert her into a carrier, but work proceeded very slowly and she was only eighty per cent complete when Japan surrendered. If she had been finished she would have been similar to the American *Saipan* carriers.

The last Japanese wartime carrier conversions to be projected were the oil tankers *Otakisan Maru*, *Shimane Maru*, *Chisusa Maru* and *Yamishio Maru* which were built in 1944, the latter two for the army. It was intended to fit them with flight decks to act as escort carriers, but early in 1945 it was decided to complete them as coal-burning cargo ships, since Japan no longer had any oil supplies; all were sunk before they could be completed.

Japan was the first country in the world to fit sonar to its carriers. Starting with *Shokaku*, all Japanese carriers completed after 1940 had passive sonar, which enabled them to detect nearby submarines and helped evasion of torpedoes. However, until the middle of the war, no Japanese carrier had radar, and in this respect the Americans, whose carriers had it from the start, had an enormous advantage. If Japanese carriers had been fitted with radar at Midway the four fleet carriers *Kaga*, *Akagi*, *Soryu* and *Hiryu* might not all have been lost, despite incompetent leadership and lack of armoured decks.

TAIHO
Displacement 29,300 tons (29,770 tonnes) normal, 33,000 tons (33,529 tonnes) full load
Length 855 feet (260 m 60 cm)
Beam 98 feet 6 inches (30 m) over flight deck
Draught 31 feet 6 inches (9 m 60 cm)
Machinery 4-shaft geared steam turbines, 160,000 shp = 33 knots
Armour belt: $2\frac{1}{4}$ to 6 inches (56 to 152 mm). deck: $3\frac{3}{4}$ inches (94 mm)
Guns 12 × 3.9-inch (100-mm) DP, 51 × 25-mm AA
Aircraft 74
Launched 7 April 1943 by Kawasaki Co., Kobe

SHINANO
Displacement 62,000 tons (62,995 tonnes) normal, 70,755 tons (71,890 tonnes) full load
Length 872 feet 9 inches (266 m)
Beam 131 feet 3 inches (40 m) over flight deck
Draught 33 feet 9 inches (10 m 28 cm)
Machinery 4-shaft geared steam turbines, 150,000 shp = 27 knots
Armour belt: $6\frac{1}{4}$ to $15\frac{3}{4}$ inches (158 to 398 mm). deck: 3 to 9 inches (76 to 227 mm)
Guns 16 × 5-inch (127-mm) DP, 145 × 25-mm AA, 12 × 28-barrelled rocket-projectors
Aircraft 47
Launched 8 October 1944 by Yokosuka Dockyard

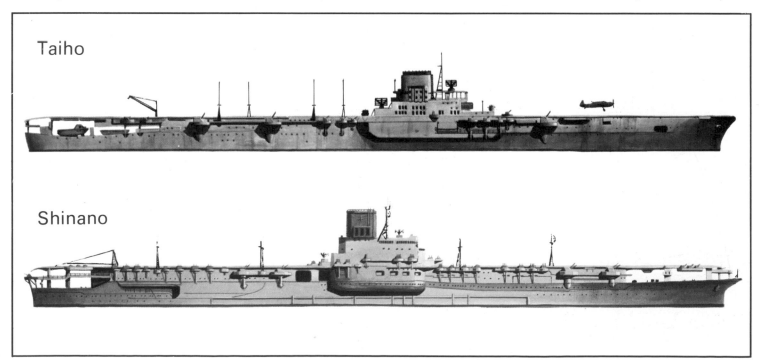

Taiho

Shinano

Capital Ships

The oldest effective Japanese battleships in World War II were the four *Kongo*-class fast battleships. *Kongo* herself had been built in Britain between 1910 and 1913 to a design that owed much to the Royal Navy, but which had been modified to suit Japanese conditions and combat experience in consultation with the major British private shipbuilders. *Haruna*, *Hiei* and *Kirishima* were built to the same design in Japan. As first completed they were lightly armoured battle-cruisers. In 1917, Britain wished to use them in the European theatre of operations, but the Japanese refused.

By the standards of the mid-1920s, the *Kongo*-class vessels were far too lightly armoured, and because Japan was unable to build any new ships under the terms of the Washington Treaty, they (except *Hiei*, which was disarmed as a training ship) were extensively rebuilt between 1927 and 1932. Torpedo bulges were fitted, one funnel was removed and the old boilers were replaced by a smaller number of new ones (though they were still coal-fired). The horizontal armour was also thickened, and the range of the 356-mm guns was extended by increasing the elevation. However the power was not increased so the speed fell by two knots to nearly 26 knots. The complicated and distinctive 'pagoda' masts fitted to these and the other Japanese battleships in the 1930s were simply the rather less tidy Japanese equivalent of the large bridges that the British and Americans fitted onto their rebuilt vessels; they had the unfortunate effect of increasing topweight very high up in the ship. Their sole advantage was the high command they gave to the forward fire control, enabling them to see the enemy at a greater range than before, but of course these massive structures could also be seen at long range by an enemy.

It was soon realized that it would be an advantage if these vessels could act as a unit with the fast fleet carriers. As originally converted they were too slow, so between 1935 and 1940 they were taken in hand again and lengthened by 7.6 m. At the same time a smaller number of oil-fired boilers replaced the first conversion's coal-fired ones; as a result the speed was raised to about 30 knots, and they were redesignated fast battleships. At the same time, 'pagoda' masts were fitted. *Hiei* was included in this rebuilding, and was brought up to the same standard as the other three. Even after the second rebuilding they were no match for a modern battleship, mainly because their armour was very weak. Japan had fully intended replacing them after the First World War with modern ships, but had been foiled by the Washington Treaty. They were, however, among the best interwar conversions, providing Japan with a much-needed and otherwise unattainable protection for the fast carriers. The weakness of their protection is demonstrated by the loss of *Hiei*, crippled in a scrappy night action off Guadalcanal by the gunfire of two cruisers and finished off by destroyers with torpedoes, and the fate of *Kongo*, sunk by a single torpedo from a submarine. Their effectiveness is shown by the speed with which *Kirishima* crippled the modern *South Dakota*, before she herself was destroyed by the radar-equipped *Washington*.

The Yamato *being fitted out in 1941. This huge vessel was the result of many years' planning; she and her sister* Musashi *were the largest World War II battleships*

45

The next class, *Fuso*, were Japan's first super-dreadnoughts. *Fuso* and *Yamashiro*, laid down in 1912 and 1913 respectively, were contemporaries of the American *Pennsylvania* ships, but whereas the American ships mounted their twelve 14-inch (356-mm) guns in four triple turrets, the Japanese were in six twin turrets. Theoretically this gave a higher rate of fire, but it also meant a longer ship with thinner armour to stretch over the greater number of magazines. In the 1930s both ships were extensively rebuilt, but without the same measure of success as the *Kongo* ships. Their horizontal armour was increased, torpedo bulges were added, the stern was lengthened by 7.6 m, and one funnel and the old boilers and turbines were removed and replaced by modern oil-burning machinery, which increased the range by one-third. However, virtually doubling the power only raised the speed by 1.7 knots. The guns' elevation was increased and a 'pagoda' mast fitted. They were too slow to be of much use in the war, and were eventually blasted to pieces by their American contemporaries in the Battle of the Surigao Straits in 1944.

Ise and *Hyuga*, laid down in 1914, were in essence improved versions of the *Fuso*-class ships, the major difference being that the two centre turrets were superimposed aft of the second funnel, instead of fore and aft of it. Their conversion between 1934 and 1937 was also virtually identical to that of the *Fuso* ships, but they were still too slow to be of any use in the carrier actions at the start of the Pacific war. Then from late 1942 to late 1943 they were both converted into carrier-battleships. Obsessed after Midway with the need to have as many aircraft carriers as possible, the Japanese wasted a valuable amount of their extremely limited shipbuilding capability on producing two hybrids whose only value was to act as bait for the American carrier planes, a role they were quite capable of performing in their original guise.

Instead of removing all the heavy armament and attempting to provide a complete flight deck, even of the crudest kind, the two aft turrets were removed and a short deck with catapults for operating floatplanes was erected in their stead, combined with an elaborate hangar and lift. The floatplanes could not land on the deck; they had to land on the water and were hoisted inboard on cranes. As it turned out, it did not matter that these two hybrids had been converted so badly, for, by the time they were ready, Japan no longer had any trained pilots to operate from them. After conversion their best feature was their heavy anti-aircraft armament.

ISE
Displacement 34,700 tons (35,257 tonnes) normal. 39,000 tons (39,626 tonnes) full load
Length 698 feet (212 m 73 cm)
Beam 108 feet 6 inches (33 m)
Draught 31 feet 9 inches (9 m 67 cm)
Machinery 4-shaft geared steam turbines, 75,000 shp = 24 knots
Armour belt: 4 to 12 inches (101 to 305 mm). deck: 7 inches (176 mm). turrets: 8 to 12 inches (203 to 305 mm)
Guns 12 × 12-inch (305-mm), 14 × 6-inch (155-mm), 8 × 5-inch (127-mm) DP, 16 × 25-mm AA
Aircraft 3 (1 catapult)
Launched 28 March 1914 by Kure Dockyard

Right: The battleship Fuso *on trials in the Bungo Straits in 1933 after her reconstruction. The 'pagoda' mast was a series of platforms built around the original tripod mast. There is a catapult on 'C' turret between the bridge and funnel. Below: The* Ise *and her sister* Hyuga *were reconstructed during 1943 with a flight deck in place of the two after 356-mm gun turrets. The drawing depicts them in 1944, by which time the floatplane had been replaced by light anti-aircraft guns, although the catapults were retained until October 1944. In 1943 the 'mattress' radar aerial was added to the control tower*

Ise

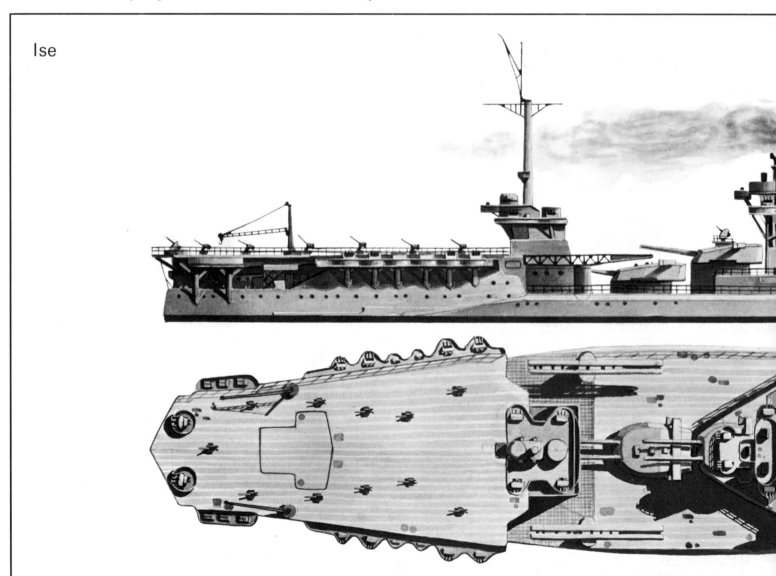

Laid down in 1916, *Nagato* and *Mutsu* were the first dreadnoughts to carry 406-mm guns. Fast, with a sensibly arranged main armament and with (for that time) moderately good armour protection, there is no doubt that they were by far the best Japanese battleship design. They were well-balanced ships, capable of taking on any foreign contemporary. Altered in the mid-1920s, they were throughly rebuilt in the mid-1930s. Horizontal armour was thickened where necessary, torpedo bulges were fitted, a funnel was removed and new engines and boilers were fitted. In addition, the hull was lengthened by 8.6 m, enabling speed to be maintained at 25 knots. The elevation of the guns was increased at the same time. Although slow by modern standards, these ships were still reasonably effective fighting units. *Mutsu* blew up in 1943 from unknown causes, the only Second World War battleship to do so, though several battleships had blown up in harbour in the First World War. Where cause could be established for these,

spontaneous ignition (usually owing to deterioration) of the ammunition was found to be the cause. *Nagato* only once took part in a surface action, at Leyte Gulf. After the war she was sunk during the second American atom bomb test at Bikini Atoll.

NAGATO

Displacement 39,130 tons (39,758 tonnes) normal, 44,000 tons (44,706 tonnes) full load
Length 738 feet (224 m 94 cm)
Beam 113 feet 6 inches (34 m 70 cm)
Draught 31 feet (9 m 44 cm)
Machinery 4-shaft geared steam turbines, 82,000 shp = 25 knots
Armour belt: 4 to 12 inches (101 to 305 mm). deck: $3\frac{1}{2}$ to 7 inches (88 to 176 mm). turrets: 14 inches (356 mm)
Guns 8 × 16-inch (406-mm), 18 × 5.5-inch (140-mm), 8 × 5-inch (127-mm) DP, 20 × 25-mm AA
Aircraft 3 (1 catapult)
Launched 9 November 1919 by Kure Dockyard

Above: The battleship Nagato *after modernization in 1936, with a 'Pagoda' mast and a single funnel. Right: The drawing depicts the* Nagato *as she was at the end of the war. Her light anti-aircraft armament had been increased from 25 to 98 25-mm guns, and air-warning and surface-gunnery radar had been added. Her sister ship* Mutsu *was lost in June 1943, after an accidental explosion in her magazines*

Nagato

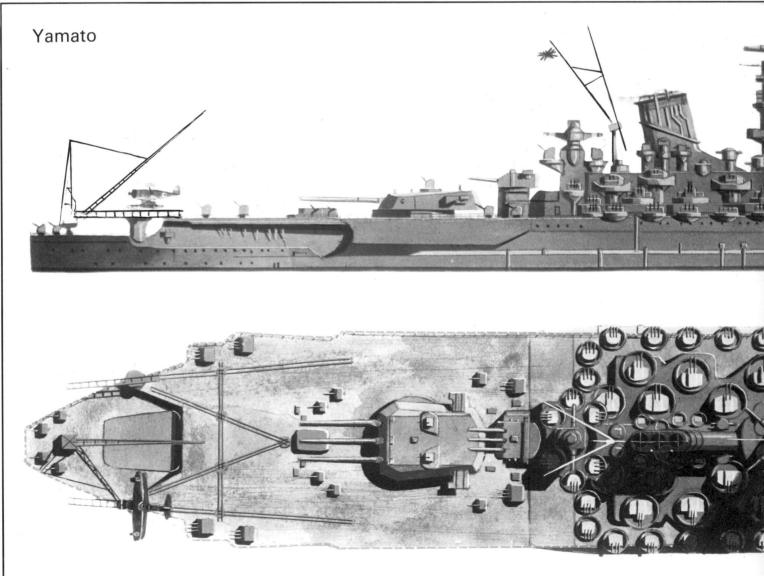

Yamato

During the later 1920s and early 1930s, Japanese naval designers refined their ideas of a battleship capable of defeating the Americans by individual superiority after producing a number of more or less credible designs. Plans for a battleship with 460-mm guns and a speed of 30 knots were called for in late 1934, on the grounds that the Americans would not build a battleship too large to go through the Panama Canal, and that any new American battleship would have a speed of 25 knots. The Japanese had calculated that the maximum size of battleship that could go through the Panama Canal would be a 64,000-tonne ship with ten 406-mm guns and a speed of about 23 knots. (It is interesting to note that both these predictions were wrong. The *Washington* class had a speed of 28 knots, and the *Montana*, though it was not built, would have been too large for the canal, as the large American carriers are today.)

The initial design to meet the Japanese naval staff's requirements would have displaced over 70,000 tonnes and was considered to be too big. Some requirement would have to be dropped, and eventually it was decided that speed could be reduced to 27 knots. By July 1936 a suitable design had been worked out. However, this was intended to be diesel powered to give a good range, and because the diesels on other Japanese warships were proving highly unsatisfactory, the design had to be reworked for steam turbines. It was just as well that this was done, because it had been intended to cover the diesels with nearly 203 mm of armour, making their extraction in case of breakdown virtually impossible.

In March 1937 the final design was prepared.

YAMATO

Displacement 64,000 tons (65,027 tonnes) normal, 69,988 tons (71,111 tonnes) full load
Length 863 feet (263 m)
Beam 127 feet 9 inches (38 m 92 cm)
Draught 34 feet 3 inches (10 m 44 cm)
Machinery 4-shaft geared steam turbines, 150,000 shp = 27 knots
Armour belt: 7.9 to 16.1 inches (200 to 405 mm). deck: 7.9 to 9 inches (200 to 228 mm). turrets: 9.8 to 25.6 inch (247 to 650 mm)
Guns 9 × 18-inch (460-mm), 12 × 6-inch (155-mm) (6 removed 1943), 12 × 5-inch (127-mm) DP, 24 × 25-mm AA
Aircraft 6 (2 catapults)
Launched 8 August 1940 by Kure Dockyard

Yamato *seen under air attack during the Battle of Leyte Gulf. The armament had been altered, with the triple 155-mm gun turrets removed and twin dual-purpose guns added*

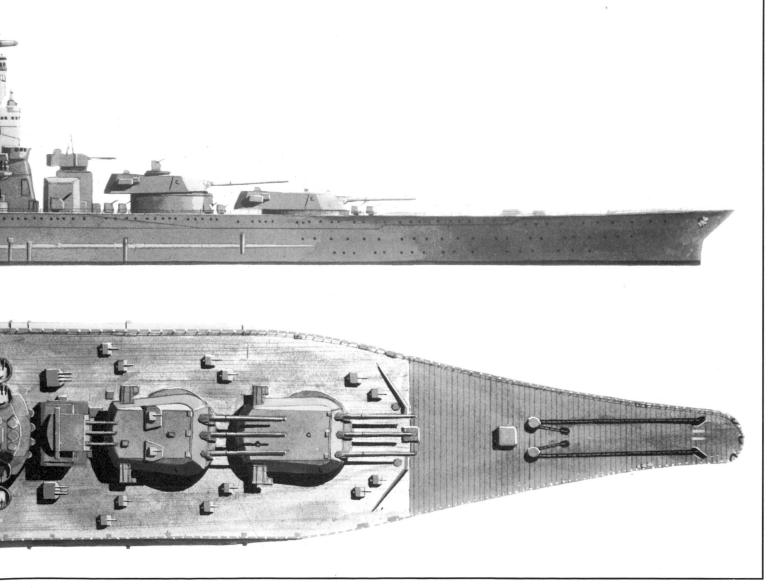

By completely ignoring the Washington and London treaties, a battleship of nearly double the treaty size was planned. But her size was to cause many problems to the designers and constructors. She had to be big; each triple 460-mm turret alone weighed about 3,050 tonnes and armour to resist 460-mm gunfire has to be very thick. However, Japanese home waters are very shallow, so the ship's depth could not exceed 8.2 m. Therefore she would have to have a large beam, which needed more power to maintain the intended speed, which itself meant more weight. Although the Japanese weight-saving methods were not as good as those used in Britain and the United States, some ingenious methods were employed.

Unfortunately for the Japanese, the damage caused by the storm during maneouvres in 1935 had shown that with the techniques they were then employing they could not trust to electrical welding for important structural members, so that method of saving weight was partially barred. However, it was possible to utilize the armour itself as a structural member, and this was done.

Another method of saving weight much favoured by the Japanese was to make the weather deck (the deck on which the superstructure is mounted) continuous, instead of breaking it in a step where a change of level was needed. This resulted in the wavy profile of most large Japanese interwar warships. This was claimed to save weight because a continuous deck is stronger than the same thickness of deck with a break in it. This is true, but when a continuous deck changes level, so much additional material is needed that frequently a broken deck line would weigh less.

As much time and trouble was taken in building the ships as in working out their design. Only one Japanese yard, Mitsubishi's Nagasaki shipyard, was large enough to build one of these ships, and even there the slipway had to be heavily reinforced to take the weight. Yet facilities were needed to build four vessels. Three yards had therefore to be built. Buildings had to be enlarged, old cranes strengthened and new ones built. A special ship was even built to transport the guns and their turrets.

In the event, only two of these battleships, *Yamato* and *Musashi*, were completed as battleships. *Shinano*, as has already been described, was converted into an aircraft carrier, and steel from the incomplete hull of the fourth vessel was used to complete other more urgently needed vessels. Yet after all this expenditure of time, money and intellect, the end results were not particularly impressive as fighting vessels. The hull form was excellently thought out – for example, the use of a very large bulbous bow helped the *Yamato* class to attain their designed speed – but the same was not true of some of the other details. Although the armour was intended to withstand 460-mm gunfire, for example, it was not realized until too late that the 155-mm gun, taken from the *Mogami* class cruisers when they were rearmed with 203-mm guns and re-used on the *Yamato* vessels, only had light armour protection. Again, the underwater protection, the effectiveness of which on any ship depends on its width, ought to have been superb, for the *Yamato* class had a greater beam than any other battleship. Yet it was not as good as it should have been. Both *Yamato* and *Musashi* took a

The battle-cruiser Hiei *is shown demilitarised to comply with the London Naval Treaty of 1932, with only three main turrets. She was brought up to standard in 1936–40*

great deal of punishment, but they were very big ships. In the end, they were both overwhelmed by a succession of small blows. This undermines the basic concept behind these ships, for in order to beat the superior numbers of American battleships, it was essential that not only should the Japanese ships have had a better armament than their opponents but that they should also have been able to withstand the greater number of hits that the superior numbers of enemy ships ought to be able to achieve. It is doubtful that the *Yamato* ships could have withstood these without impairing their own fighting capabilities, and because there were bound to be fewer of them than of their American opponents, any losses the Japanese sustained would make the situation of the remaining ships that much worse. No other country seriously considered building such ships; Germany produced mere pipedreams, and even the American *Montana* class, much better balanced ships, would have been 5,000 tonnes smaller. Even without hindsight about the deadliness of carrier-borne aircraft, ships of this size were too vulnerable to a greater number of smaller ones to warrant gambling such a large proportion of a country's design effort and, even more important, shipbuilding capacity, on them.

Two battle-cruisers of 33,000 tonnes with nine 311-mm guns and a speed of 33 knots were ordered, but because of the overriding need for carriers, they were cancelled in 1942.

Cruisers

The earliest Japanese interwar light cruisers, laid down in the First World War, were based on, though not exact copies of, the British 'C' class light cruisers. These were the *Tenryu* class, whose design was then developed into the *Kuma* class.

In 1927 they were all fitted with a catapult, and when the Japanese adopted the 610-mm torpedo as standard instead of the 530-mm they all mounted 610-mm torpedo tubes. This was the 'Long Lance' 610-mm torpedo powered by oxygen, which had a range of 22 km at 48 knots and 40 km at 36 knots. It was not introduced until 1938, and destroyers did not receive it until 1941. However, when its potential was recognized, it was decided to fit two cruisers with large numbers of this deadly long-range weapon. Therefore *Oi* and *Kitakami* were converted in 1941 into torpedo cruisers, retaining four 140-mm guns, but with the entire midsection taken up with ten quadruple 610-mm torpedo tube mounts. Various armament changes were made to all these ships during the war, and *Kitakami* was eventually fitted with four 127-mm guns and 67 25-mm dual-purpose anti-aircraft guns. In addition she was fitted to carry and launch while under way eight *Kaiten* one-man torpedoes. The six ships of the *Nagara* class and the three of the *Sendai* were progressive developments of the *Kuma* class. Built in 1923, the same year as the *Sendai*-class ships, with the same speed. Slightly cruiser designed with the Washington Treaty in mind. On a displacement of 2,950 tonnes she mounted the same armament as the 5,280-tonne *Sendai* class ships, with the same speed. Slightly larger than the French *Contre Torpilleurs*, she was built like a large destroyer. In fact, she was too small and too lightly built, but she did mark the start of several Japanese attempts to build lightweight cruisers.

The next attempt, the two ships of the *Furutaka* class, which were completed in 1926, had an armament of six 203-mm guns in light-weight gun-houses with a speed of 34 knots on a displacement of 8,120 tonnes. These were the first Japanese ships to use side armour as longitudinal strength girders. They were rebuilt in 1937–38 with twin gun-mountings, rotating torpedo tubes and 120-mm instead of 76-mm anti-aircraft guns. The ships were now much more efficient fighting ships, and the displacement was now well over 9,000 tonnes – very near to the 10,160 tonnes of other countries' 203-mm cruisers – with eight guns, much better seaworthiness and better arranged protection. However, although they were lightly built, these ships could absorb a considerable amount of damage. The *Aoba*, an improved version of the *Furutaka* class, was not sunk until the last days of the war, despite being seriously damaged several times. The two *Aoba* ships introduced the twin 203-mm mounting and the 120-mm gun, and the rebuilt ships of the *Furutaka* class were very similar.

The *Myoko* class of heavy cruiser stopped trying to get round the terms of the treaty by using lightweight techniques. Instead, the four members of this class were large powerful ships with an armament of ten 203-mm guns arranged in twin turrets, three forward and two aft, a disposition later copied by the Americans in their *Brooklyn*-class light cruisers. The *Myoko* class were well armoured, and had a speed of nearly 34 knots. This basic design was used for most of the remaining Japanese interwar cruisers.

It is not surprising that these ships come out well of a comparison with other treaty cruisers, for these '10,000 ton' cruisers flagrantly ignored the treaty tonnage limitations by displacing nearly 13,400 tons (13,600 tonnes).

The next class, *Takao*, *Atago*, *Chokai* and *Maya*, were virtually the same as the *Myoko* class, having a somewhat larger bridge and 25 mm thicker side armour. The torpedo tubes were moved from the main deck to the upper deck in this class so as to obviate the possibility of the

The heavy cruiser Mikuma *seen from an American aircraft after sustaining heavy damage during the Battle of Midway. On the wrecked rear turret can be seen the remains of an American Vindicator dive-bomber. She was sunk by air attack the following day, but her sister* Mogami *escaped with similar damage*

ship being sunk if the torpedoes exploded in their tubes. *Chokai* was always part of the Combined Fleet, often being used as fleet flagship, and her armament was never altered. All the other members of the class were modernized; *Maya* had her third 203-mm turret replaced by two 127-mm anti-aircraft turrets after bomb damage in 1943. These ships all had large bridges so they would have the space and accommodation necessary for them to act as flagships if required. In subsequent Japanese cruisers the size of bridge was reduced.

In order not to exceed the numerical limits set by the Washington Treaty, the next class were armed with 155-mm guns and classed as light cruisers. However, this was something of a misnomer, for the two original ships of the *Mogami* class, *Mogami* herself and *Mikuma*, were only slightly smaller versions of the *Takao*. As first built they were unstable, for too much lightening had been attempted on the electrically welded hull, and the triple turrets, which were disposed differently from those in the *Takao* and *Myoko* classes, added weight high up. They entered service in 1935, and in 1936 were rebuilt with bulges and had their hulls strengthened. Between 1939 and 1940, the triple 155-mm turrets were replaced by twin 203 mm, as they were on their slightly later sisters, which had received the hull modifications while under construction. These 155-mm triple turrets were later fitted to the *Yamato*-class battleships. Despite their inauspicious introduction into service, this class proved capable of absorbing a tremendous amount of damage, as both *Mogami* and *Mikuma* showed at Midway. Although *Mikuma* eventually sank, *Mogami* survived for two more years. These were the first Japanese light cruisers built since the First World War not to have the handworked 140-mm gun, adopted because its 36-kg shell

was easier for the usually small Japanese seaman to lift than the 45-kg 155-mm one. With power-worked turrets such considerations no longer applied.

The *Mogami* class were the first of a large number of 155-mm cruisers in Japan, Britain and America which were, in all but gun calibre, heavy cruisers. The next Japanese class designed to take 155-mm guns were the *Chikuma* and *Tone*. With the later *Oyodo*, they were unique among modern cruisers in having all their main armament forward. They were completed with 203-mm guns, mounted in four twin turrets all forward of the bridge. Aft of the superstructure was a flight deck designed to carry five reconnaissance seaplanes.

These were the last large Japanese cruisers to be completed. The following class, the three *Katori* ships, *Kashii*, *Kashima* and *Katori*, were built as training ships for seamen, and they were intended for ocean cruising. A fourth was laid down in August 1941, but she was cancelled after the outbreak of war, and the material was used for other ships. The three ships of the *Katori* class were used as fleet flagships during the war. In 1944 *Kashii* and *Kashima* were converted for anti-submarine work. They were comparable with the French *Jeanne d' Arc* and the Argentinian *La Argentina*.

In the late 1930s it was realized that when the 155-mm cruisers were given 203-mm guns, Japan would have no modern light cruisers. In any case the *Mogami* class were too large to work with destroyer flotillas. Therefore the Japanese built the four *Agano*-class light cruisers. Completed between 1941 and 1944, they were excellent examples of their type, if a little under-armed, with a high speed of 35 knots, but they were no longer of much use in the type of carrier warfare being waged in the Pacific.

An enlarged and modified version, *Oyodo*, was

intended to act as the flagship for a group of submarines, with a speed of 36 knots, no armour, two triple 155-mm turrets forward, and a large hangar and catapult astern to carry and launch six high-speed reconnaissance floatplanes. The planes were never built and so the ship lacked a purpose. Early in 1944 the hangar was converted into accommodation, the large catapult replaced by a smaller one, and the ship was used as the Combined Fleet's flagship.

A start was made in 1942 on two heavy cruisers which were to be modified versions of the *Mogami* class. *Ibuki* was intended to be completed as an aircraft carrier, though this was never finished, and her unnamed sister was cancelled almost as soon as work began. Two more fast cruisers were ordered in 1942, but they too were soon cancelled.

CHOKAI
Displacement 11,350 tons (11,532 tonnes) normal, 13,100 tons (13,310 tonnes) full load
Length 668 feet 6 inches (203 m 75 cm)
Beam 61 feet 4 inches (18 m 69 cm)
Draught 20 feet (6 m)
Machinery 4-shaft geared steam turbines, 130,000 shp = 35½ knots
Armour belt: 3 to 4 inches (76 to 101 mm). deck: 1½ to 5 inches (38 to 127 mm). turrets: 1½ inches (38 mm)
Guns 10 × 8-inch (203-mm), 4 × 4.7-inch (120-mm) AA, 12 × 25-mm AA
Torpedo Tubes 8 × 24-inch (610 mm).
Aircraft 2 (2 catapults)

Above right: The heavy cruiser Furutaka *after reconstruction in 1938, with twin 203-mm turrets replacing the single mountings. Right: The heavy cruiser* Chokai *in April 1939. Chokai, unlike other ships in her class, was not altered, and spent most of the war serving as a flagship for the Japanese combined fleet*

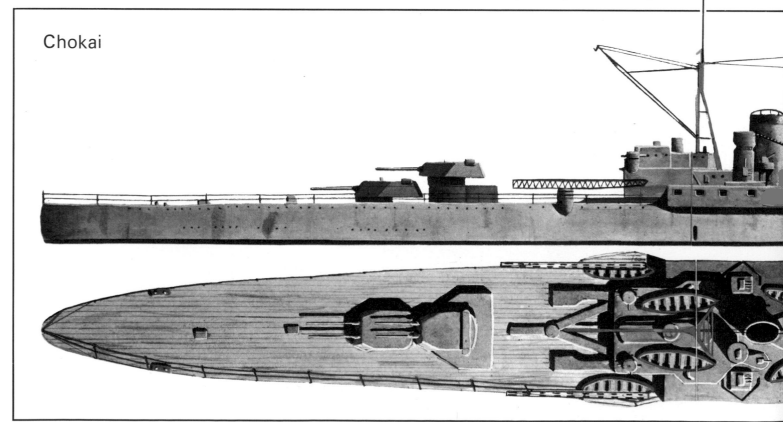

Chokai

Destroyers

The first Japanese interwar destroyers were the ships of the *Momi* class, which with their torpedo tube mounting set in front of the bridge were heavily influenced by German designs. Of 782 tonnes displacement, an armament of three 120-mm guns, two twin 530-mm torpedo tubes, and a speed of 36 knots, they were classed as second-class destroyers, as were their slightly improved successors, the *Wakatake* class. Both these classes were extensively used in Chinese coastal waters, for which their shallow draught made them ideal.

Their first-class equivalents were the *Minekaze* and *Kamikaze* classes, displacing just over 1,220 tonnes with an extra 120-mm gun and pair of torpedo tubes. The *Minekaze* ships were particularly fast, the designed speed being 39 knots. In late 1944, *Namikaze* of this class was badly damaged by a mine, and was reconstructed as a *Kaiten* human torpedo carrier. The stern was cut down to the waterline so they could be discharged when the destroyer was under way. *Shiokaze* was later altered for the same purpose. The *Mutsuki* class were improved *Kamikaze*-type vessels, and they introduced the 609-mm torpedo, mounting it in two sets of triple tubes.

The next destroyer design marked a complete break with the previous designs. In 1925, with the need for individual Japanese warships to be superior to their opponents because of the 5:5:3 warship ratio, the Japanese naval staff asked for a destroyer displacing only 1,670 tonnes with a maximum speed of 38 knots, and an armament of three twin 127-mm guns and three triple 610-mm torpedo tubes, with reloads. The result was the *Fubuki*-class 'Special Type' destroyer, a great advance on previous types. The longer, higher, flared forecastle, which now extended to the bridge, gave much-improved seaworthiness. The 127-mm gun turrets were mounted one forward and two aft, an arrangement used in most subsequent classes. The very heavy torpedo armament reflected the excellence of the Japanese 610-mm torpedo, even before the oxygen-driven version came into service, making it into a significant long-range weapon.

Naturally, cramming so much armament onto so small a hull had its drawbacks, the chief of which was that they were rather unstable, a condition not improved by the fitting of a heavier dual-purpose turret on the later ships in the class instead of the original low-angle gun. After the damage caused by the storm of September 1935 – in which *Hatsuyuki* of this class had her bows wrecked up to the bridge – more ballast was fitted and the hull was greatly strengthened. Displacement rose to nearly 2,130 tonnes, speed dropped by four knots to 34 knots, and a clearer comparison could be made with foreign designs that had been drawn up with more care for hull strength and seaworthiness and less for evading treaty limitations.

The best features of the later members of this class were shown to be not the ability to carry a large armament on a limited displacement, but the heavy torpedo armament and the dual-purpose main armament, a feature that many nations intended to incorporate in their designs, but which most did not install in their destroyers until the late 1930s. During the war one of the 127-mm turrets was removed to enable the anti-aircraft armament to be improved. Only one damaged ship survived the war, and most of the destroyer classes had few, if any, survivors. They were used too intensively in the front line for any number to escape the eventual crushing weight of American sea and air superiority.

The last four members of the first 24 'Special Type' destroyers had three more powerful boilers to replace the original four, and they incorporated other detail improvements. The last one to be completed, *Hibiki*, which entered service in 1933, was the first totally rivetless ship in the Imperial Japanese Navy.

The London Treaty of 1930 further limited the numbers and individual size of the destroyers that the Japanese, and other navies, could build. Because of this, more 'Special Type' destroyers could not be built for some time, and so an attempt was made to design a destroyer of equal firepower but on a displacement of only 1,420 tonnes. Only one 127-mm gun was eliminated, and the torpedo armament remained the same as in the *Fubuki* class. In addition, this new class, *Hatsuharu*, comprised the first Japanese destroyers to be fitted with reloading gear. This

could be used at sea, and effectively doubled the torpedo armament at the cost of added top-weight, vulnerability, and less available deck-space. The Japanese, with their excellent torpedoes, concluded that the advantages outweighed the extra problems, whereas other navies, with less effective torpedoes, mostly disagreed.

Since the larger ships in the *Fubuki* class had proved unstable, it was not surprising that the *Hatsuharu* vessels, with virtually the same top-weight on a smaller hull, were even worse in this respect. The first two to be completed were drastically altered: the armament was reduced and modified, one triple torpedo mount and its reload facilities were taken out, the superstructure, masts and funnels were lowered, and extra ballast added. As a result, speed fell by 3.5 knots. The remainder of the class were completed in this modified form. The follow-on class, *Shiratsuyu*, were completely redesigned. These ships incorporated all the modifications found necessary in the earlier class. Apart from a smaller bridge and different funnels, the chief difference between the classes lay in the introduction of quadruple torpedo tubes. Thus only two mountings were now necessary to fire the minimum of eight torpedoes in a salvo that the Japanese considered necessary to ensure a hit.

The *Asashio* class which followed were very

Below: A Japanese destroyer of the Minekaze *class, whose design was strongly influenced by German practice. This contrasts with the* Fubuki *(bottom), the first purely Japanese design and one that had great influence in other countries. The* Fubukis *had heavy dual-purpose gun armament, exceptionally heavy torpedo armament, and high speed*

similar, but had one more 127-mm gun, bringing the number back up to six, and slightly increased power and speed. Their turning circle proved unexpectedly large, and this was rectified by fitting a different-shaped stern, which also increased the speed slightly. The machinery, too, gave problems initially, though these were cured by late 1941.

The end of treaty limitations marked a return to 2,030-tonne destroyers; indeed the *Kagero* class were basically *Fubuki* ships improved by incorporating all the developments tested in the intervening classes. Except for the poor sonar and the lack of radar, this class was as good as any in the world. Unfortunately for the Japanese, these exceptions were of vital importance in the almost exclusively air and undersea war of the Pacific. In the few surface actions that took place, these destroyers performed very satisfactorily. In the end, most of the surviving members of this and the other Japanese destroyer classes were lost acting as fast transports, trying to succour the cut-off Japanese garrisons on the various Pacific islands. The only member of this class to survive the war, *Yukikaze*, suffered no casualties and was not hit once, despite being in front-line service throughout the war. One ship, *Amatsukaze*, was experimentally fitted with high-pressure boilers. As with most surviving Japanese destroyers, 'X' turret was removed in 1943–44 to make way for an increased anti-aircraft armament.

The next class, *Yugumo*, were almost identical to the *Kagero*, but the ships had a modified bridge, were fitted with radar, and had their 127-mm guns' elevation increased from 55° to 75°, giving much better capability.

The need for fast anti-aircraft escorts to provide close cover for aircraft carriers was realized well before Japan entered the war, and the *Akitsuki* class, the first of which were ordered in 1939, were designed to fill this role. Before the first ships were completed in 1942, it had been decided to endow them with some degree of surface and anti-submarine capability as well. When completed, the armament of these handsome and effective vessels consisted of four twin 100-mm anti-aircraft turrets, a number of light anti-aircraft guns, one quadruple 610-mm torpedo tube mounting, and six depth-charge throwers and 72 depth charges. These were large ships, with a displacement of 2,730 tonnes and a length of 122.7 m overall, and their speed was 33 knots. They were most closely akin to the somewhat larger cruisers of the *Dido* and *Atlanta* classes, used by the British and American navies respectively. Unfortunately, by the time the *Akitsuki* ships came into service most of the carriers they had been intended to protect had already been sunk. Half of them were eventually cancelled.

Apart from the experimental *Shimakaze*, which had high-pressure boilers and was also the first Japanese destroyer to have a quintuple torpedo tube mounting, the last Japanese wartime destroyers were the *Matsu* and simplified *Matsu* classes. Ordered in 1943 and 1944, when Japanese destroyer losses had become catastrophic and the large destroyers were taking too long to build, these were a greatly simplified 1,220-tonne design with a relatively heavy surface armament and a speed of only 28 knots. In speed and armament they greatly resembled the British 'Hunt' class, and they were designed for

ease of production because numbers rather than performance were now essential. Despite this they performed very well, and the arrangement of engines and boilers so that the aft engine room was between the two boiler rooms helped to ensure their survival. In 1943 an even simpler design was prepared, but none of the ships of the simplified *Matsu* class were completed when the war ended. These vessels helped make up the catastrophic pre-war shortfall in anti-submarine escorts.

In addition to the destroyers, there were two classes of fast torpedo boat built in the 1930s to take advantage of the lack of treaty restriction on vessels of this type of under 610 tonnes. Like their French equivalents they were extremely unstable and unseaworthy, too much having been attempted on the displacement. It was the capsizing of *Tomodzuru*, one of these ships, in 1934 that first showed how unwise it was to try and beat the treaty restrictions by piling too heavy an armament on too small a hull – a lesson that the Japanese were rather slow to profit from.

YUKIKAZE
Displacement 2,033 tons (2,065 tonnes) normal, 2,400 tons (2,438 tonnes) full load
Length 388 feet 6 inches (118 m 41 cm)
Beam 35 feet 6 inches (10 m 81 cm)
Draught 12 feet 4 inches (3 m 75 cm)
Machinery 2-shaft geared steam turbines, 52,000 shp = 35 knots
Armour none
Guns 6 × 5-inch (127-mm) DP, 4 × 25-mm AA
Torpedo Tubes 8 × 24-inch (610-mm) (16 torpedoes carried)
Launched 24 March 1939 by Sasebo Dockyard

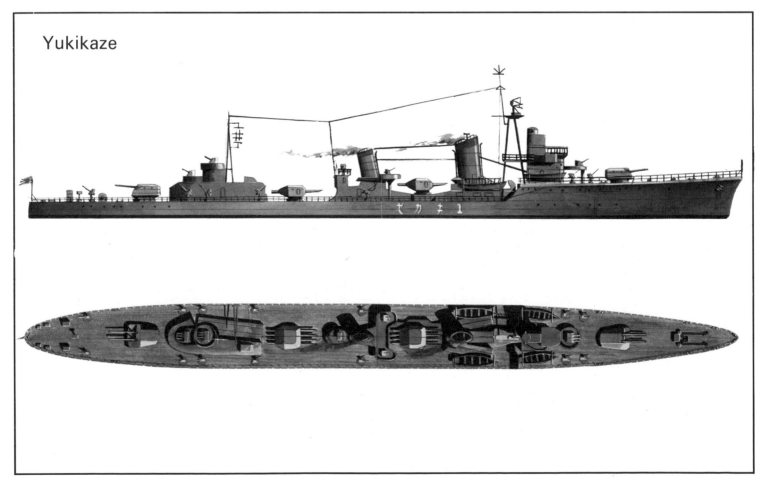

Yukikaze

Submarines

Japan had a sizable submarine force at the beginning of the war. Well handled, it ought to have achieved considerable results. Although some successes were achieved early in the war, particularly against the American carriers, the end results were disappointing. Poor doctrine, with an overemphasis on attacking warships, resulted in an almost total failure to disrupt any of the US invasion fleets that were gradually mopping up Japanese conquests in the Pacific. Then the Japanese submarines were frittered away in a vain attempt to provide sufficient men and materials to keep the Japanese garrisons in being. Used as transports, they lost their chance to permanently discourage the American advance. Although the Japanese submarines were by no means the best in the world, they were quite good enough to have given Japan a chance to achieve stalemate, if they had only been properly employed.

Almost all the Japanese interwar submarines were of two main types. First there were the *Kaidai*-type submarines, mostly of about 1,620 tonnes surface displacement, with a radius of action of over 16,000 km and a surface speed of over 20 knots. These were intended to take part in fleet actions, hence the high surface speed. The other type were intended to act as long-range scouting submarines, and had an even greater radius of action and a surface displacement of over 2,030 tonnes. The later versions also carried aircraft. The first type was developed from British, German and French designs, while the latter was very directly developed from the large German First World War cruiser submarines. The first one to be fitted with an aircraft (not, initially, very successfully) was *I 5*, launched in 1931.

Odd men out were the *I 121* class. Practically identical to the German First World War *U 125*, they were smaller and slower than most of the other Japanese submarines completed in the late 1920s. In 1940 these four submarines were fitted with external petrol tanks to refuel the main fleet's floatplane reconnaissance aircraft.

Another odd class were the two 710-tonne surface displacement submarines of the *RO 33* class, launched in 1934 and 1935. In the late 1930s, Japan developed a successful midget submarine, and several of the large scout submarines were adapted to carry them. Their only success in the war was the torpedoing of HMS *Ramillies* in Diego Saurez harbour.

When war became imminent a new type of coastal submarine, the *RO 100* class of 533 tonnes surface displacement, were hastily developed. They were intended for close defence of Japanese outposts and home waters, and they had a very restricted radius of action of 5,800 km while surfaced. Only one more medium-sized attack submarine class was built by the Japanese Navy. These were the *RO 35*s. Eighteen were built between 1941 and 1944 and a further 28 were cancelled in 1943. These submarines were of 975 tonnes surface displacement and had a radius of action of 8,050 km. American success in destroying Japanese submarines forced the Japanese to abandon active submarine warfare. The only submarines built after this were

coastal transport and large cruiser submarines, both of which were intended for highly specialized roles.

The *I 361* class of supply submarines were intended for running supplies to invested island garrisons, for which purpose they could carry 82 tonnes of cargo and two landing craft on the coaming aft of the conning tower. Towards the end of the war, they were modified (as were many

Three Japanese submarines lie moored alongside the American submarine tender Proteus *after the surrender in September 1945. On the left are the sister vessels* I 400 *and* I 401, *the largest submarines in the world at that time. On the right is the* I 14, *also large even though it was only two-thirds the size of the* I 400s. *Note the aircraft catapult and hanger which can be seen on each of the boats*

surviving Japanese submarines) to carry *Kaiten* human torpedoes.

These boats were succeeded by the slightly modified *I 373*s, which could carry up to 260 tonnes of cargo. Both the *I 361*s and the *I 373*s were armed but the last type of transport submarine, the *Ha 101* class, were intended purely to carry cargo, and on a surface displacement of 375 tonnes they could carry 60 tonnes of cargo for 4,800 km. They were intended for ease of production and some of them were completed in five months. The building of all remaining types of submarine other than these and suicide craft was discontinued in March 1945 so as to expedite their construction.

Despite the urgent need for large numbers of submarines during the war, the Japanese persisted in building specialized craft. The most famous of these were the very large submarines of the *I 13* and *I 400* classes. The *I 13*s were the largest submarines that the Japanese had built up to that time. On a surface displacement of 2,635 tonnes they carried an armament of one 140-mm and seven 25-mm guns, six 530-mm torpedo tubes and two aircraft. The surface speed was 16 knots and they had the immense radius of action of 21,000 miles (39,000 km). Ordered in 1942, it had been intended that these should be cancelled because of American successes against the large Japanese submarines. However, Admiral Yamamoto issued a direct order that they should be continued, and two were completed in 1945.

The *I 400* class were also only built because

of a direct order from Admiral Yamamoto. Over half as big again as the *I 13*s, these were the world's largest submarines at the time when they were built. They were intended to fulfil all the Japanese submarine's designed roles except that of transport. Their aircraft were intended to be used to attack the Panama Canal. The most peculiar feature of their design was the shape of their hull. In order to keep the draught as shallow as possible the hull was constructed as two side-by-side cylinders. They were fitted with a *schnorkel*, and were sometimes fitted with a dummy funnel as a disguise when sailing on the surface in home waters.

Quite apart from the vulnerability of these large submarines, there was no excuse for wasting a large amount of shipbuilding capacity on their construction, for this capacity was needed for vessels much more important to Japan's survival. There was some excuse for wasting time and effort on the *Yamato* class, for no one knew how soon war would be declared, or even if there would be a war at all. The building of the *I 13*s and the *I 400*s did not even have this justification.

In 1937 a small highly streamlined experimental submarine, *No 71*, was laid down in Japan and on test she achieved the underwater speed of 21.25 knots. After the tests were completed she was scrapped in 1940. This marked a breakthrough in submarine design. Although her underwater endurance was limited, she came close to being a true submersible. In 1943 the first of the *I 201* class, which were based

on the results of *No 71*, were laid down. These antedated the German Type XXI submarines and had an underwater speed of 19 knots, which they could maintain for 55 minutes.

In 1943 and 1944 the Japanese Army also built a number of transport submarines, the *Yu 1* class and the slightly larger *Yu 1001*s, which were built so that the army could supply its own garrisons without needing to call upon the navy for assistance.

The last underwater craft built in Japan in the closing stages of the war were an immense number of small suicide craft, intended to slow down, if not to turn back, the anticipated American invasion. Very few of these were ever used in action.

I 400
Displacement 5,223 tons (5,306 tonnes) surfaced, 6,560 tons (6,665 tonnes) submerged
Length 400 feet 3 inches (121 m 99 cm)
Beam 39 feet 4 inches (11 m 98 cm)
Draught 23 feet (7 m)
Machinery surfaced: 2-shaft diesel-electric, 7,700 bhp = 18¾ knots; submerged: 2-shaft electric, 2,400 shp = 6½ knots
Guns 1 × 5.5-inch (140-mm), 10 × 25-mm AA
Torpedo Tubes 8 × 21-inch (532-mm) (20 torpedoes carried)
Aircraft 3 (1 catapult)
Launched 1944 at Kure Dockyard

Top: The submarine I 53, *a vessel of the KD3A class, renumbered* I 153 *in 1942. She was built in 1925–27. Right:* Kairyu *suicide craft after the surrender*

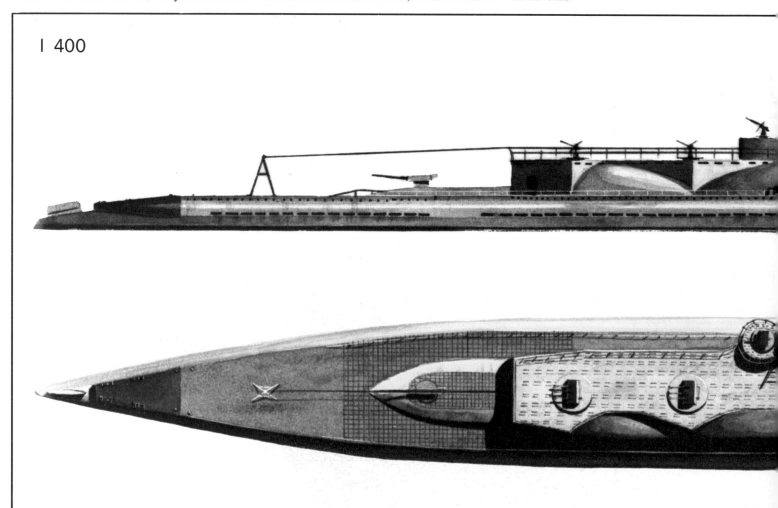

I 400

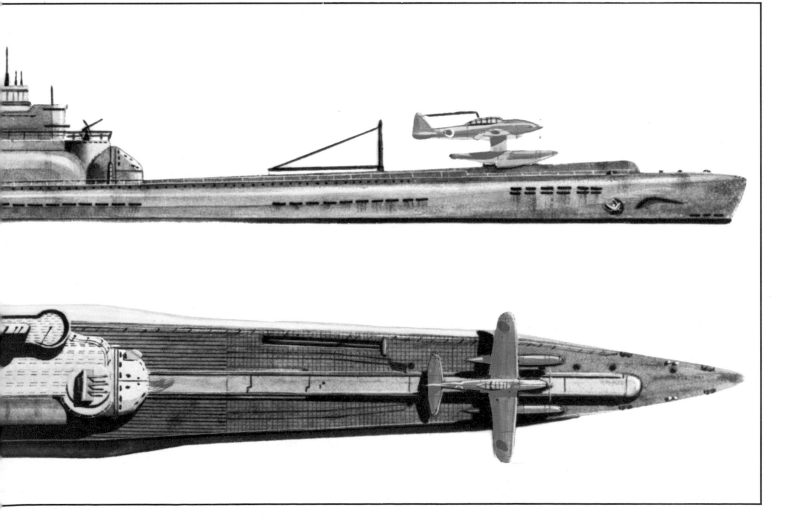

GREAT BRITAIN

The Royal Navy in 1939 was not only the largest in the world but also had the longest continuous existence, the finest fighting reputation, and the greatest series of successes. Its reputation for seamanship and competence was legendary and most other navies to a greater or lesser extent copied the RN's uniforms, customs and organization. Though the end of the war saw the Royal Navy surpassed in size by the US Navy, it saw no diminution of the older navy's reputation. Despite disasters the fighting record of the Royal Navy was good, and Allied victory owed much to its far-off storm-beaten ships.

Behind the Royal Navy was the largest mercantile marine in the world, and behind both naval and merchant fleets the biggest shipbuilding industry. British shipbuilders might lag behind other countries in their adoption of some modern techniques, but they still built very fine ships, and few could rival them in expertise. To cite one example, the *Leander*-class cruisers were built in about half the time taken by French yards for the *Galissonniere* class of comparable size.

Like the Royal Navy, British designers were expert and reliable, and their experience was second to none. One of the oldest principles of British warship design was that a large number of good ships was better than a few brilliant ones. This made great sense in the light of both history and geography, for Britain was an island and had for centuries been the dominant European naval power; whether fighting France or Germany her overseas trade was a matter of life and death to her. Her ships had to be ready to meet attack at all times, while her enemies could attack when they chose; numbers rather than individual strength was therefore the answer. When an enemy did appear the Royal Navy would rely on better training, morale, and the possibility of reinforcements coming. Usually this formula worked, as when *Ajax*, *Achilles* and *Exeter* wore down the *Graf Spee* at the River Plate on 13 December 1939, or when Admiral Vian's small cruisers and destroyers held off an Italian battleship and heavy cruisers at the Second Battle of Sirte.

The combination of this rationally worked-out, though historically based, design doctrine with the effects of the naval treaties, which the Royal Navy observed more scrupulously than some others, was to ensure that most British ships designed between the wars were somewhat smaller and less spectacular than their foreign contemporaries. The cruisers were slower than

Italian vessels and less heavily gunned than the Japanese, but they were to prove adequate and well-balanced fighting ships. Seaworthiness, adequate protection, good gun control, habitability, long range and many other qualities, not visible on first inspection, were given due weight in most British designs. Indeed, Admiralty requirements on stability and structural strength were held to be overdone by most other navies.

British designers had the inestimable advantage of having had much practical experience in the effectiveness of their designs during the First World War, when several rude lessons had been administered. They also had full access to the records and experience of the German Navy which had administered those lessons, for the British took over most of the German naval records after the armistice in 1918. The result of being able to combine the records of both navies' war experience with an unbroken series of experiments and designs between the wars was that the British produced far more effective schemes of internal protection for their battleships than the Germans – effective, that is, in enabling the battleship to continue fighting after damage.

On the whole, British ships were sensibly designed for a task, rather than specifically to overmatch individual foreign contemporaries. There might have been a slight tendency to conservatism, to hanging onto the well-tried and reliable rather than experimenting with the new and initially unreliable; usually the British let others do the initial experimenting and proving before they took over a new invention. However, there were enough examples of radical innovation in the Royal Navy from the *Dreadnought* to the first aircraft carriers to prove this generality to be very much less than an absolute rule.

The Royal Navy did have its failures and deficiencies. Like most other navies before the war its attention to the perils of aircraft attack had been inadequate and misdirected. Though far from unaware of the danger, the RN still underestimated it: too few of the smaller ships had any heavy high-angle guns at all, while light anti-aircraft guns were totally inadequate in numbers and not much better in quality. The dire effects of prolonged Royal Air Force control over the quality of Fleet Air Arm aircraft – though not aircrew – will be considered in more detail when we come to the aircraft carriers. In the early years of the war, RN damage-control standards were somewhat behind the best German and American ones.

As the war went on, and thanks to excellent shipyard organization and resources, many of the deficiencies were rectified. When *Luftwaffe* attack showed the deficiency in anti-aircraft guns the ubiquitous Bofors 40-mm and Oerlikon 20-mm guns were adopted. They replaced the totally inadequate multiple 0.5-inch (12.7 mm) machine-gun, and supplemented the multiple pom-pom, whose excellent rate of fire was not matched by its range. Radar sets were added, so that the British, behind the Germans in seaborne radar until 1941, thereafter rapidly drew ahead. American aircraft were supplied to British carriers and new weapons such as 'Hedgehog' and 'Squid' developed to deal with submarines.

The famous Warspite *bombards German shore positions in 1944. The superimposed turret aft (X turret) had been damaged by a glider bomb at Salerno and could never be used again*

Aircraft Carriers

The aircraft carrier was developed in Britain, as were the earliest techniques of deck landing. Yet in 1939 Britain had the least effective naval air arm of the three major powers which possessed this vital addition to naval strength. This had nothing to do with the quality of British aircraft carriers, arguably the best and certainly the most thoroughly designed in the world. Certainly it also had nothing to do with the quality of the aircrew. The Fleet Air Arm was superbly trained, and indeed had to be: 'They say in the Air Force a landing's okay/if the pilot he gets up and walks right away/but in the Fleet Air Arm the prospects are dim/if the landing is poor and the pilot can't swim,' as one song put it. It was in the quality and quantity of the aircraft available that the Royal Navy fell behind the Americans and Japanese.

The basic reason for this was the decision on April Fool's Day 1918 to found a separate air force. At one blow not only was the navy deprived of its air arm – which was not returned to naval control until 1937, far too late to rectify the years of neglect – but also of most of its air-minded officers. The RAF, intent on preserving its independence, paid little attention to developing its seaborne forces, while the Navy tended to concentrate on developing spotting aircraft which might be able to manage a torpedo attack as a sideline. The worst deficiency of all was the failure to produce a carrier-borne single-seat fighter capable of matching its land-based contemporaries. When war came the Royal Navy's carriers had to rely on obsolete aircraft such as the Swordfish, converted landplanes like the Seafire, American imports like the Wildcat, Hellcat and Avenger, or home-produced oddities like the Barracuda. It was not until after the end of the war that the first really adequate British carrier fighter, the Sea Fury, entered service.

Despite these handicaps, British carriers and their aircraft more than justified themselves. Fleet Air Arm Skuas, operating from an airfield, bombed the German cruiser *Königsberg*, the first major warship sunk by air attack. A tiny force of obsolete Swordfish achieved the most economical victory of the war, crippling the Italian fleet in its base at Taranto, while fighters helped to preserve convoys and defend landings in the Mediterranean.

At the outbreak of the war nearly all British carriers were built on hulls which had not only been constructed during the previous conflict, but also were not originally designed for operating aircraft. Three had been conceived as light battle-cruisers, designed for use in a far-fetched scheme to land troops in the Baltic. Two of these, *Courageous* and *Glorious*, originally had two twin 15-inch (380-mm) turrets each, and were converted to aircraft carriers in the 1920s. Both were sunk early in the war, and had little chance to prove themselves. The third ship, *Furious*, was intended to carry two 18-inch (457-mm) guns. In the event only one was fitted, and a flying-off deck fitted forward. This was used for the first-ever carrier landings, but was obviously inadequate. Soon a landing-on deck was built aft, in place of the 18-inch (457-mm) gun. However, the funnel and bridge structure

were obviously unnecessary excrescences in the middle of the ship, and so *Furious* was completely rebuilt with a completely flush flight deck. There was a small retractable navigating bridge but nothing else stood out above the flight deck, the smoke being ejected through vents below deck level aft. This was not the last alteration to this much-changed ship, as she was rebuilt and modernized just before the Second World War.

Two smaller carriers came into service just after the end of the First World War. One, *Argus*, had been built as a passenger liner, and was given, like the *Furious*, a flight deck with nothing sticking out above it. However, she did not have the bigger ship's speed, and was mainly used for training and ferrying tasks during the later conflict. The second ship, *Hermes*, was much more interesting, being the first carrier designed and built as such. Unlike *Furious* and *Argus* she had an 'island', incorporating the bridge and funnel, offset to one side of the ship; this was a more sensible solution to the problems of accommodating the command facilities of the ship and getting rid of the boiler gasses. Unfortunately *Hermes* was a small and relatively slow ship, and could only carry a few aircraft. The last of the older generation of aircraft carriers was the *Eagle*, built on a hull which was to have been a Chilean battleship. She, too, had an island, but was unusual for a carrier in having two funnels. Like the *Hermes* she was rather slow for a carrier, but sturdy.

The first of the new carriers built during the years of rearmament in the 1930s was the *Ark Royal*. A great deal of thought and research went into her design, and that of her successors. The British were most thorough, and took great care over the aerodynamic design of the island and flight deck to avoid eddies in the air-flow which might endanger aircraft landing and taking off. British carriers also had much better precautions against fire and protection of aviation fuel supply lines than their American and Japanese equivalents. All this went into the *Ark Royal* as well as a powerful anti-aircraft armament of 4.5-inch (114-mm) guns. Purely as a carrier of aircraft she was the best equipped of all the wartime British carriers, thanks to her two-level hangar, which gave her a capacity equivalent to the big American carriers. If she had not been lost comparatively early in the war, due to poor damage control, she could have taken advantage of wartime developments in aircraft stowage to carry even more.

The later British fleet carriers had a much smaller aircraft complement because of their exceptionally good protection. It has often been said that the best feature of the *Illustrious* class was their armoured flight decks. This is not the whole truth, as some of all nation's major carriers had flight deck armour, although the British ships had the thickest. What distinguished the *Illustrious* and her sisters was that the whole hangar, the most vulnerable area of the ship above the waterline, was enclosed in an armoured box. In the context of the time when these ships were designed this was a wise decision. These carriers were going to operate in the Mediter-

ranean and North Sea with fighters of inferior performance against superior enemy air forces. With the early warning facilities given by radar, and the better carrier fighters that came later, the balance between greater weight of armour and more aircraft (the *Illustrious* class only had a single hangar deck against the *Ark Royal*'s two) might have been different. As it was, the *Illustrious*'s survival against massed *Stuka* attacks and heavy bomb damage in the Mediterranean in 1941 proved the decision a sensible one. Later, radar and a good combat air patrol of fighters gave equally good protection against conventional air attack, as the Americans proved in the Pacific. However, towards the end, the British armoured carriers came into their own again when they continued operating against a scale of *kamikaze* attacks which disabled several American carriers for a long time.

It is interesting that even before this experience the Americans were impressed enough by

ILLUSTRIOUS
Displacement 23,207 tons (23,579 tonnes) standard, 28,619 tons (29,078 tonnes) full load
Length 743 feet 9 inches (226 m 69 cm)
Beam 95 feet 9 inches (29 m 18 cm)
Draught 24 feet (7 m 31 cm)
Machinery 3-shaft geared turbines, 111,000 shp = 30½ knots
Armour belt: 4½ inches (114 mm). deck: 4½ inches (114 mm) hangar side, 1½ to 3 inches (38 to 76 mm) flight deck
Aircraft 36
Guns 16 × 4.5-inch (114-mm) DP, 6 × 8-barrelled 40-mm pom-poms
Launched 5 April 1939 by Vickers-Armstrong, Barrow

Eagle, Formidable *and* Indomitable *escort the allied* Pedestal *convoy in August 1942*

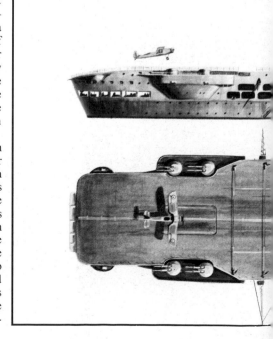

Illustrious

the British design to offer to exchange some of their *Essex*-class carriers for an equal number of British fleet carriers. The British, for their part, equally impressed by the American ships' aircraft capacity, were prepared to take part in the exchange. However, for a variety of reasons, this exchange, which had been seriously discussed in 1943, never came off.

Illustrious had two sisters, *Victorious* and *Formidable*. The fourth ship of the class was the *Indomitable*, but her design was modified so that she became in effect the prototype of two more ships, *Implacable* and *Indefatigable*. In order to take account of the criticisms of the small number of aircraft carried by her predecessors, *Indomitable* was given an extra half hangar deck aft, below the main hangar. To compensate for this extra weight the armour on the hangar sides was made thinner. Originally the two final ships were to have had a full-length lower hangar deck, but as the capacity for aircraft stores and armament would have been inadequate for so many planes, they were only given a half hangar, like *Indomitable*.

Because of stability problems all three of these later ships had less height in their hangars, which meant that there were types of aircraft that could not be operated by them. Also, after the war, as aircraft size continued to grow, it was the earlier ships that were kept in service. The first four ships had a triple shaft installation, new to British major warships, and one that gave

considerable trouble, whereas *Implacable* and *Indefatigable* had four shafts.

Considered purely as ships rather than as platforms for operating aircraft these British fleet carriers were the best of their type built, and it is significant that many of their best features, the built-up bow and armoured hangars especially, were adopted by the Americans in their later construction. However, the transatlantic flow of information was not all one-way, and the British adopted the superior American flight-deck operation techniques, as well as American aircraft. They were also considering putting deck-edge lifts, an American concept, into their biggest carriers, the *Malta* class, which were never built, though two other large carriers, *Ark Royal* and *Eagle*, were completed after the end of the war.

Although the six ships of the *Illustrious* group were the only British major fleet carriers completed during the war, other, smaller carriers were built. Besides the escort carriers which we will consider later, there were the light fleet carriers. These had mercantile hulls with a view to converting them to merchant ships after the war was over (none were, in the event); they carried only close-range anti-aircraft guns and no armour, but were otherwise small versions of the fleet carriers. Unfortunately, they were completed too late to play a part in the war, but subsequently proved a very effective concept. They have been sold or given to a wide variety

of navies, and several are still in service.

One very useful smaller ship was being built before the war began, though not completed until 1943. This was the *Unicorn*, designed as an aircraft maintenance ship, but capable of acting as an ordinary carrier at a pinch, which she did, with some success, in the Mediterranean in 1943. Later she proved so useful in her designed role with the British Pacific Fleet that two of the light fleet carriers then being built were converted for the same purpose.

INDOMITABLE
Displacement 24,680 tons (25,076 tonnes) standard, 29,730 tons (30,207 tonnes) full load
Length 754 feet (229 m 81 cm)
Beam 95 feet 9 inches (29 m 18 cm)
Draught 25 feet (7 m 61 cm)
Machinery 3-shaft geared turbines, 111,000 shp = $30\frac{1}{2}$ knots
Armour belt: $4\frac{1}{2}$ inches (114 mm). deck: $1\frac{1}{2}$ inches (38 mm) hangar side, $1\frac{1}{2}$ to 3 inches (38 to 76 mm) flight deck
Aircraft 48
Guns 16 × 4.5-inch (114-mm) DP, 6 × 8-barrelled 40-mm pom-poms, 8 × 20-mm AA

The aircraft carrier Indomitable *in the Indian Ocean in 1942. British fleet carriers differed from the* Essex *class of the US Navy in having an enclosed 'hurricane' bow and the 4.5-inch (114-mm) guns at the four corners of the flight deck*

Indomitable

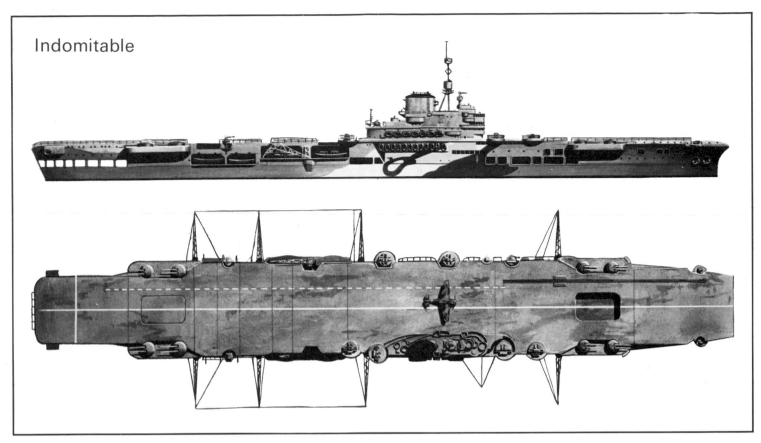

The German's most dangerous attack on Britain was the attack on her maritime communications. The possibility of defeat in the Battle of the Atlantic was the one which scared Churchill the most. The chief enemy was the U-boat, but the depredations of long-range bombers, the Focke-Wulf Condors, were also a serious threat. Air cover was needed, especially as aircraft proved to be getting the highest score of submarines sunk. Long-range patrol aircraft were in very short supply early in the war because of the demands of the strategic bomber offensive against Germany. It was not until 1943 that aircraft were provided which could cover the entire North Atlantic convoy route from shore bases.

Meanwhile another answer to the problem of air cover for the convoys had been tried successfully. This was to provide aircraft carriers for the purpose. Fleet carriers were too few, too vitally needed elsewhere, and too precious to use in this role. Therefore the possibility of building smaller aircraft carriers for escort purposes was examined. The possibility of mercantile conversions had been discussed before the war, but mainly in terms of the largest liners (especially the *Queen Mary* and the *Queen Elizabeth*). These proved to be too valuable in their role as troop transports and so smaller and slower ships were chosen.

The trial conversion was, ironically, a captured German ship. The *Hannover* was a brand-new diesel ship captured at the beginning of the war, and at first named *Empire Audacity*. Her superstructure was cut down and a simple wooden flight deck fitted; this was a fairly rudimentary conversion, with no lift or hangar, so that aircraft had to be stowed and serviced on deck. As she was primarily intended to provide cover against aerial shadowers and

EMPIRE FAITH
Displacement 7,061 tons (7,174 tonnes) full load
Length 431 feet (131 m 36 cm)
Beam 57 feet 5 inches (17 m 49.5 cm)
Machinery 1-shaft diesel, 688 shp = 11 knots
Guns light AA only
Launched 4 March 1941 by Barclay Curle, Glasgow

Empire Faith

Audacity

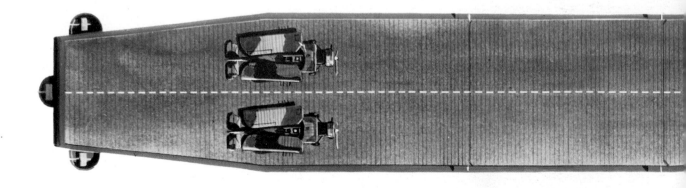

bombers the six aircraft she carried were all Grumman Martlet fighters (the English name for the Wildcat). Completed in mid-1941, she was immediately put on the Gibraltar convoy run.

Audacity was torpedoed and sunk before the year was out, but not before she had proved how invaluable even the smallest carrier could be. Condors had been shot down and U-boats harried by her aircraft. British yards were too occupied to do more than a few escort carrier conversions, and these were generally rather too elaborate, but the basic ideas were passed over to the United States, which soon started to produce escort carriers for itself and the British in large numbers. These designs will be discussed in greater detail in the American section, but it may be worth noting that a considerable amount of inter-Allied friction was caused by British delays in putting their American-built escort carriers into service because of their insistence on more stringent safety precautions.

The British eventually received some 39 escort carriers from the Americans, but many of these were diverted to other purposes, especially the support of amphibious landings. The need for integral air support for convoys remained, however, and the 'MAC' ships were evolved to meet this need. These were reasonably fast merchant ships, either grain ships or oil tankers, which did not need large hatches to load their cargoes, and could therefore have a flight deck added without impairing their ability to carry a cargo. They were manned by the Merchant Navy, not the Royal Navy, except for the aircraft contingent. The oil tankers had six obsolescent Swordfish, the grain-ships only four (the Swordfish was one of the few aircraft which could take off from their very short flight decks) but the grain-ships had the advantage of a lift and a small hangar. These ships were more like the *Audacity* than the later elaborate escort carriers, but arrived a little late to play a vital part in the Battle of the Atlantic, which had to a great extent been won before they arrived.

In the desperate days of 1941 any expedient which provided some degree of air cover to convoys was better than none, particularly one which provided some protection against other aircraft. This desperate need produced the 'CAM' ships, of which *Empire Faith* was one. These were the Catapult Aircraft Merchantmen, which carried a single Hurricane fighter on a catapult forward. This was a one-shot weapon. Once catapulted the pilot could only 'ditch' in the sea, or bale out when his petrol ran out, hoping to be picked up by the convoy escorts. If he was lucky enough to be near to land he might be able to fly to a land base, but in any event the aircraft was no longer any use to the convoy. Obviously the moment to catapult the fighter had to be chosen with great care if it was to achieve worthwhile results. The method was expensive in scarce fighters and in even scarcer pilots, and also expensive in the ships themselves. Over one-third were lost, so it is not surprising that the 'CAM'-ship concept was dropped as soon as numbers of escort carriers became available.

However, they did have a certain value: some German aircraft were shot down, and their presence exercised a beneficial effect on the morale of the convoys and dissuaded German aircrews from attacking. The 'CAM'-ships, and also the Fighter Catapult Ships, which were naval auxiliaries fitted with catapults and naval fighters, were only stopgaps, but they fulfilled this function properly. When looking at the illustration of the *Empire Faith* it should be remembered that the artist has shown her rather high out of the water; in normal service, even unladen, her decks would be far nearer the waterline.

AUDACITY
Displacement 10,200 tons (10,363 tonnes) full load
Length 467 feet (142 m 34 cm)
Beam 56 feet (17 m)
Draught 18 feet (5 m 48 cm) mean
Machinery 2-shaft diesels, 4,750 bhp = 16 knots
Armour none
Aircraft 6
Guns 1 × 4-inch (102-mm) AA, 6 × 20-mm AA

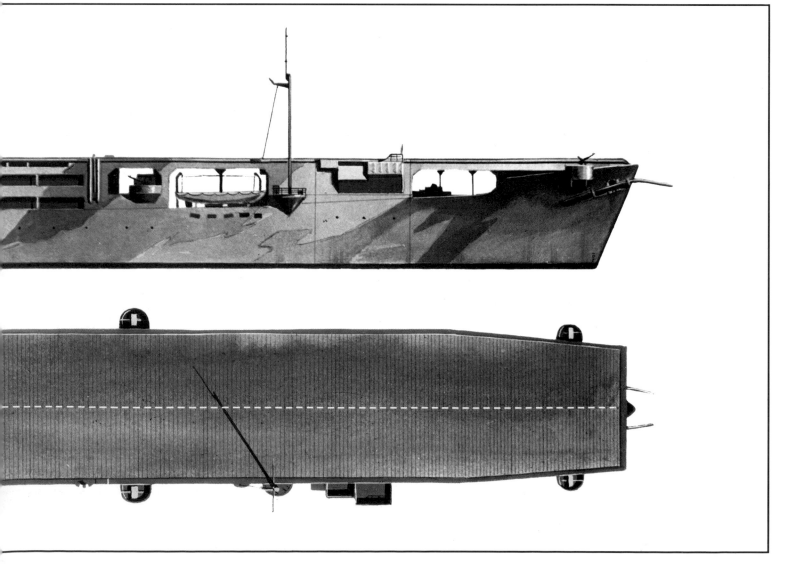

Capital Ships

Hood *seen after her last refit with new twin 4-inch (102-mm) a/a mountings*

At the beginning of the war the Royal Navy had a numerically powerful force of battleships. They were, however, all quite old. The majority had served in the First World War and some remained virtually unaltered since those days. Others had been heavily altered. The *Nelson* and *Rodney* were the only battleships in the world

incorporating the full lessons of the First World War, but they were no longer in the first flush of their youth, and rather slow by current standards. The first of Britain's new class of battleships, the *King George V*, was still fitting out.

Three of Britain's capital ships were, strictly speaking, not battleships at all, but battle-cruisers. This was a type developed by the Royal Navy before the First World War in an attempt to extend the capabilities of the largest cruisers,

the armoured cruisers, by giving them a battle-ship's gunpower, while retaining cruiser speeds and standards of protection. This was an unfortunate move, as it proved, because it meant that the ships would be treated as fast battleships when they were not capable of standing up to a proper battleship's fire, and their speed would not always be sufficient protection. The fact that the three British battle-cruisers lost at the Battle of Jutland blew up due to inferior cordite and poor magazine-stowage arrangements, rather than thinner armour, does not really affect this argument. Jutland initiated a reaction against the battle-cruiser, though two 15-inch (380-mm) ships – the *Repulse* and *Renown* – were at a too advanced stage to cancel. Both were altered between the wars and given more protection; the *Renown*, indeed, was almost completely rebuilt just before war broke out and she had a very distinguished career in the war. Neither, however, were really considered to be a match for a battleship, especially as they only had six 15-inch (380-mm) guns apiece.

This view, however, was modified for their immediate successor, the *Hood* – for a long time the largest warship in the world, and the most handsome capital ship ever built. There were originally to have been four ships of her class,

Hood

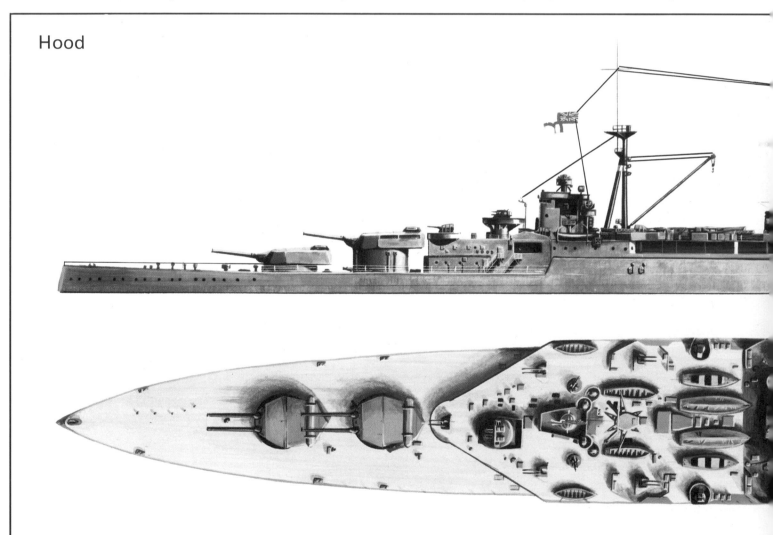

designed before Jutland was fought but modified after that battle to incorporate considerably more protection, and thereby losing some freeboard – becoming lower in the water – and two knots in speed from the original target of 33 knots.

The other three ships were cancelled before the end of the First World War but *Hood* was completed despite the misgivings of the new chief designer – the Director of Naval Construction, Sir Eustace Tennyson D'Eyncourt – because it was felt that she would have some experimental value. But it should not be thought that the *Hood* was badly protected. The alterations to her had produced what was in effect a fast battleship rather than a battle-cruiser. She was at least as well armoured against bombs and shells plunging down on her – an increasing danger thanks to the great range at which actions were fought – as contemporary battleships such as those of the *Queen Elizabeth* class. Her armour was, however, spread over a wide area of her hull, and therefore comparatively thin, whereas by 1918 it was becoming increasingly obvious that armour should be concentrated to protect the really vital points – a system already adopted by the Americans and called 'all or nothing'. The *Hood* also had the disadvantage of her

enormous length, necessary for her original great designed speed and the powerful engines and boilers which that speed required.

By 1939 *Hood* was overdue for a complete rebuild, but this was prevented by the outbreak of war. By the time of her loss in 1941 she had been changed from her original appearance. Her unusual original secondary armament of single 5.5-inch (140-mm) guns had been removed, and instead five of the ubiquitous twin 4-inch (102-mm) anti-aircraft gun mountings were substituted. The main armament, eight 15-inch (380-mm) guns in mountings slightly different to those in the other British ships of the same generation, was retained. On top of B turret (immediately in front of the bridge) and also between the 4-inch (102-mm) mounts were the oddly-shaped tubes of a rather useless anti-aircraft weapon. This was a rocket projector which was a stop-gap until enough light anti-aircraft guns could be produced. Thanks to the increase in weight of the ship she lay noticeably deeper in the water, so that in any sort of a sea, or at speed, the low-lying quarterdeck was usually awash. Her top speed was less than 30 knots by then, but she was still a useful unit.

It was her bad luck that the superb gunnery of the *Bismarck* found one of her weaknesses so

early in the Denmark Strait action. Unfortunately her torpedo tubes, which were situated above water, had been left undisturbed by refits. It can never be known for sure just why she exploded and sank, but the *Bismarck*'s hit was amidships, and the fire which started there possibly set off the torpedoes. This seems more likely to have caused the catastrophe than the rocket or 4-inch (102-mm) ready-use ammunition – or a penetration of the magazines which should not have been pierced or set off with such ease.

HOOD

Displacement 42,100 tons (42,775 tonnes) standard, 46,200 tons (46,941 tonnes) full load
Length 860 feet 6 inches (262 m 28 cm)
Beam 105 feet 3 inches (32 m)
Draught 28 feet 6 inches (8 m 68 cm)
Machinery 4-shaft geared steam turbines, 144,000 shp = 31 knots
Armour belt: 5 to 12 inches (127 to 305 mm). deck: 1½ to 2 inches (38 to 51 mm). turrets: 11 to 15 inches (280 to 380 mm)
Guns 8 × 15-inch (380-mm), 10 × 4-inch (102-mm) AA, 3 × 8-barrelled (40-mm) pom-pom AA, 4 × 4-barrelled MGs
Torpedo Tubes 4 × 21-inch (530-mm) above water
Launched 22 August 1918 by John Brown, Clydebank

The oldest operational battleships in the Royal Navy were the famous *Queen Elizabeth* class. The ships of this class were the finest battleships of the First World War, several knots faster than any of their predecessors, and the first ships designed to take the superlative twin 15-inch (380-mm) mounting. This gun deserves a special mention on its own account. After World War II the US Navy conducted a thorough comparison of all heavy gun mountings; the conclusion was that despite the fact that it was old, that it did not have the range or the weight of shell of 16-inch (404-mm) or 18-inch (457-mm) mountings, its accuracy, rate of fire and the simplicity and reliability of its mounting more than made up for this.

Because of their speed and power the class were used as a special fast squadron of their own, co-operating with the battle-cruisers. For a while at Jutland they virtually took on the German High Seas Fleet singlehanded, and gave out and received a considerable amount of punishment. During the 1920s the handsome silhouette of the class was altered for the worse by trunking back the foremost of the two funnels into the after one; more significantly, external bulges were added against torpedo attack. Two of the

class, *Barham* and *Malaya*, were left basically in this state when war broke out, though with the addition of extra anti-aircraft guns and a seaplane catapult. Like the 'R' class battleships (see next section) these two were not altered much during the war, and *Barham* was finally lost to a submarine's torpedo.

The *Warspite* was refitted at Portsmouth between 1934 and 1937, and what emerged from this process was virtually a new ship. The turrets were retained, but with 10° more elevation which gave them greater range. The armour was also kept, though there was a considerable amount of extra horizontal protection added on the decks. A block-like tower bridge replaced the old armoured conning tower and multiple-layer bridge. The whole interior of the ship was gutted and new boilers and engines put in. These gave more power for less weight, and the boiler uptakes could be led to a single funnel. The 6-inch (152-mm) secondary armament in its old-fashioned casemates in the hull was still retained, but was supplemented by 4-inch (102-mm) anti-aircraft guns in twin mounts, and by the formidable but short-ranged eight-barrelled pom-poms.

Armour plate and guns and gun mountings

were the most difficult parts of a new battleship to produce, and took the longest time. Because the immediate need for ships fit to meet modern conditions was so pressing in the late 1930s, the conversion of the *Warspite* was probably justified, despite the time and money required. These were not far off the requirements for a new ship, which would, in the long run, have been a better investment. In the circumstances, though, and in view of the *Warspite*'s magnificent war record, one can hardly complain. Sent in to Narvik Fjord in a calculated risk, her heavy salvoes smashed the German destroyers trapped there. Later she fought the Italians as Admiral A B Cunningham's flagship, most notably at the Battle of Matapan. Hit by a glider bomb off Italy, she was patched up to serve at the bombardments of D-Day and Walcheren.

Her two other sisters, *Queen Elizabeth* and *Valiant*, had even more elaborate refits. They had their 6-inch (152-mm) batteries removed and were fitted instead with countersunk 4.5-inch (114-mm) twin high-angle mountings similar to those fitted in *Renown* and the *Illustrious* class of carriers. Like *Warspite* these two battleships had distinguished war records, and were continually altered to take new anti-aircraft guns

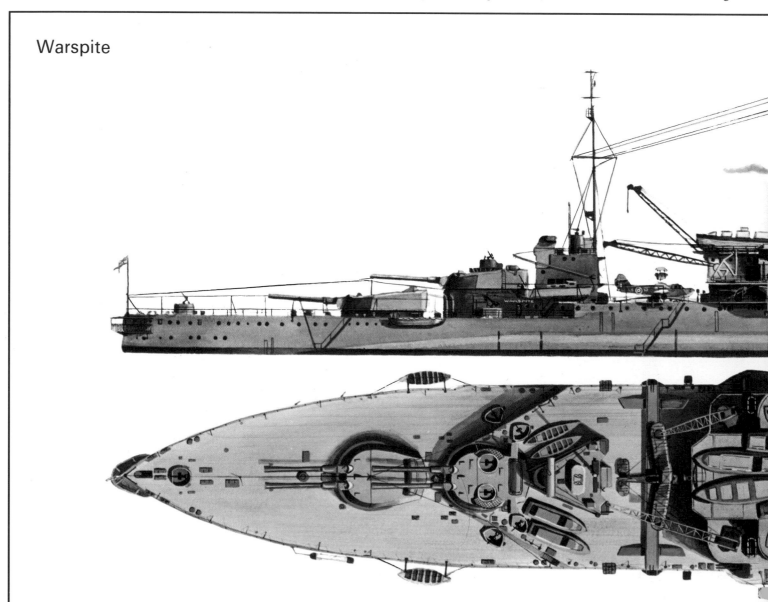

Warspite

and radar; unlike her, both suffered from the attentions of Italian human torpedoes in Alexandria Harbour and had to be refitted in the USA.

The *Queen Elizabeth* class will continue to exert a fascination on everyone who loves large warships. No other twentieth-century battleship combined such drastic alterations with distinguished service in both world wars.

WARSPITE
Displacement 30,600 tons (31,091 tonnes) standard, 34,500 tons (35,053 tonnes) full load
Length 643 feet 9 inches (196 m 21 cm)
Beam 104 feet (31 m 69 cm)
Draught 30 feet 9 inches (9 m 37 cm)
Machinery 4-shaft geared turbines, 80,000 shp = 24½ knots
Armour belt: 8 to 13 inches (203 to 330 mm). deck: 1¼ to 3 inches (31 to 76 mm). turrets: 5 to 13 inches (127 to 330 mm)
Guns 8 × 15-inch (380-mm), 8 × 6-inch (152-mm), 8 × 4-inch (102-mm) AA, 4 × 8-barrelled 40-mm pom-poms
Torpedo Tubes removed
Launched 26 November 1913 at Devonport Dockyard

Quadruple 2-pounder pom-pom guns of the type fitted in British warships

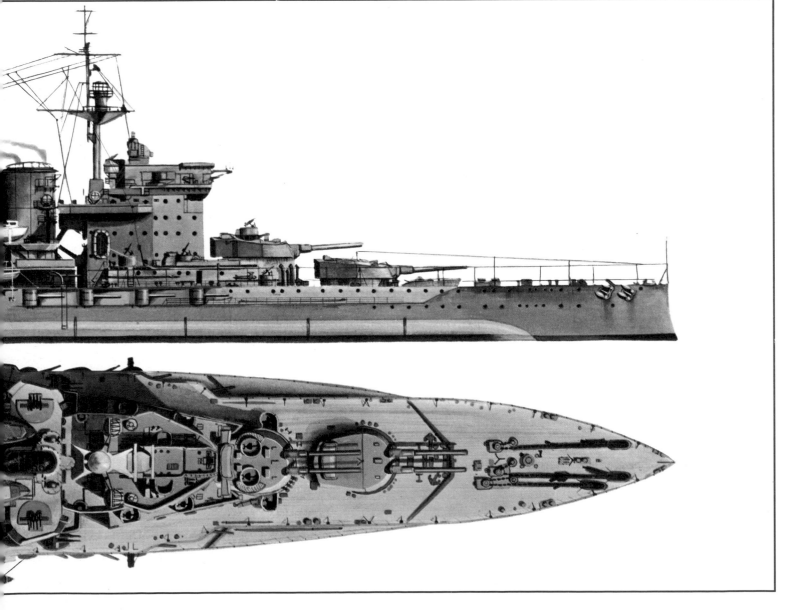

Although slightly later than the *Queen Elizabeth* class, the five ships of the *Royal Sovereign* class did not receive the complete rebuilds of the three ships previously referred to. This was mainly because the 'Rs', *Revenge, Resolution, Royal Oak, Ramillies* and *Royal Sovereign*, were shorter and slower. They were an excellent design when they were conceived at the outbreak of the First World War. They carried the same armament as the *Queen Elizabeth* class, but were originally intended for coal fuel (this was changed to oil while they were being built) and were given less stability, which meant that they were steadier gun platforms. Because of this reduced stability the armour protection was raised higher in these ships; this meant that it would be less likely for a shell hit to start flooding.

All in all, the 'Rs' were an excellent design for their day, sturdy, powerfully armed, with a handsome pyramidal appearance and single

Royal Oak *at the outbreak of war, with an added aircraft catapult and modern a/a guns*

Royal Oak

capped funnel. By 1939 they were all obsolescent and due for retirement. Refits during the inter-war period had added bulges against submarine attack, installed seaplane catapults and augmented the anti-aircraft armament, but basically they were not altered much. Almost certainly the decision not to rebuild them was wise, as the resources which this would have taken were better employed in building new ships. This is not to say that the 'Rs' were useless; far from it, though they could only be considered as second-line battleships. They were vulnerable to air attack because of their lack of horizontal protection, even after the usual wartime light anti-aircraft guns had been added, so they had to be kept away from enemy bases. They were not really a match for a modern enemy battle-ship, but could be usefully employed in guarding convoys, where an enemy raider might well shy away from another capital ship, however old and weak. This was in fact what happened several times during the war when German heavy ships avoided action with British convoys because of

the presence of an old battleship. At a pinch the old 'R' ships could be added to a fleet, as happened in the desperate days of 1941–42. In this employment, however, their age told against them; they were plagued with minor breakdowns and could not make their nominal full-load speed of 21 knots. A more sensible employment was shore bombardment, which is how most of the class ended their active careers. One, *Royal Sovereign*, was transferred on loan to the Russians in 1944 as the *Archangelsk*. She was returned after the war in a dreadful state, covered in rust, all her guns loaded with live ammunition and much of it rusted in place.

The ship illustrated, however, did not survive long enough to build any sort of fighting record during the Second World War. On 14 November 1939 the German submarine *U-47* managed to penetrate the unfinished defences of Scapa Flow and her second salvo of torpedoes sank the *Royal Oak*. A minor mystery is why no one apart from the anxious submariners heard the bang of one of the dud torpedoes exploding but the result is

not in doubt; allegations of sabotage seem improbable when it is known that *U-47* was inside Scapa Flow, and did fire two salvoes of torpedoes. The *Royal Oak* herself still rests on the bottom of the Flow, undisturbed because she is officially held to be a war grave for the large number of her crew who went down with her.

ROYAL OAK
Displacement 29,150 tons (29,617 tonnes) standard, 33,500 tons (34,037 tonnes) full load
Length 624 feet 3 inches (190 m 27 cm)
Beam 102 feet 6 inches (31 m 24 cm)
Draught 28 feet 6 inches (8 m 68 cm)
Machinery 4-shaft steam turbines, 40,000 shp = 22 knots
Armour belt: 6 to 13 inches (152 to 330 mm). deck: $1\frac{3}{4}$ to 2 inches (45 to 51 mm). turrets: $4\frac{1}{4}$ to 13 inches (108 to 330 mm)
Guns 8 × 15-inch (380-mm), 12 × 6-inch (152-mm), 8 × 4-inch (102-mm) AA, 2 × 8-barrelled 40-mm pom-poms
Torpedo Tubes 4 × 18-inch (456-mm) above water
Launched 17 November 1914 at Devonport Dockyard

After the end of the First World War all the lessons of that war were taken into account, as well as the findings from experiments with captured German ships. The result was a series of original designs culminating in the 'G3' design which was ordered, but then cancelled as a result of the Washington Naval Treaty. This class would have had high speed and strong protection, both in armour (which would have been on the 'all or nothing' principle) and in a system of internal bulges against torpedo attack. These magnificent ships would have looked very odd, with all the gun armament forward, but with the first two triple 16-inch (406-mm) turrets separated from the third by the bridge. They would, however, have been more than a match for any of the Japanese or American ships being built at the time, and would have been at least equal in fighting power to the much later *Bismarck*.

The design appeared in a modified and reduced form in the *Nelson* and *Rodney*, smaller and much slower ships, but still with excellent protection, which included special arrangements against underwater damage which worked excellently when tested by action damage in the Second World War. These two ships had all three main turrets in front of the bridge, making them look rather like immense angry oil tankers. They also had their secondary armament 6-inch (152-mm) guns in twin turrets on the upper deck; this proved to be a successful innovation.

The Admiralty deliberately played down the less visible aspects of this original and successful design, and the ships have never been given enough credit. In all respects except speed (they could only do 23 knots) they were the equals of much later foreign designs. It must, however, be admitted that the 16-inch (406-mm) was not as successful a gun or mounting as the earlier 15-inch (380-mm); the guns wore out much faster, and had more than their fair share of teething troubles.

British battleship design did not stop short with *Nelson* and *Rodney*. A whole series of studies were made in the years between the wars, but financial stringency and the provisions of treaties prevented anything coming of them till the mid-1930s when the threats of Japan, Italy, and rearming Germany were becoming too obvious to be ignored. The result was the building of the *King George V* class, of which *Howe* was a later example. Like *Nelson* and *Rodney*, this class, the only recently designed British battleships to serve in the Second World War, have perhaps been given less than their due as designs. They did not appear to be very spectacular ships, and this aesthetic impression was reinforced by the fact that they carried a smaller calibre of gun than any foreign equivalent. This was because their design was prepared at a time when the naval treaties still held sway, and the Admiralty suspected that new ships might be restricted to 14-inch (356-mm) guns. An adequate design of gun from the First World War period was adapted, and the Admiralty decided to compensate for the slight loss in range and hitting power by carrying more guns. (Stories that the 14-inch (356-mm) was a brand-new design which mysteriously possessed superior qualities to other navies' 15-inch (380-mm) or 16-inch (406-mm) guns were just a propaganda 'blind'.) Originally the new class was to have

carried 12 guns in three quadruple turrets, but the increasing need for heavier protection on the decks against long-range shelling and bombs led to one quadruple turret being dropped in favour of a twin to save weight.

The quadruple turret had been first adopted by the French, and another innovation in the new British class had also appeared first in the *Dunkerque* class. This was the merging of the secondary anti-destroyer armament with the tertiary anti-aircraft armament in one high-angle/low-angle gun. The *King George V* class had a twin 5.25-inch (133-mm) gun, a rather complicated mounting and rather too heavy for effective anti-aircraft fire. However, the idea was a good one, and later became standard.

Where the *King George V* class shone in comparison with their foreign contemporaries was in their heavy, simple and effective armour protection. This, particularly the horizontal armour, was heavier than in any foreign equivalent. The US Navy, which had invented the 'all or nothing' system, did not armour its later ships particularly heavily (most published figures on this are wrong). The British disposition of protection was far more sensible than that of the *Bismarck*; despite legends to the contrary, British armour was at this time equal in quality to German (as was proved in comparative trials after the war) and thicker.

The *King George V* class turned out to be an effective design when they were tested in action. There was a lot of teething trouble with the quadruple 14-inch (356-mm) mountings, particularly noticeable in the *Prince of Wales* when she met the *Bismarck* before she was fully worked up. But what is often ignored by commentators on this action is that the German battleship and *Prinz Eugen* would have had a great problem in trying to 'finish off' the British ship as so many have suggested they should. Because of faults in the mountings the *Prince of Wales* would not have been able to make much of a reply to the German fire, but her powerful protection was intact, her machinery functioning, and her only serious hit was by a German shell on the bridge – a shell which, incidentally, did not explode. She would have been very difficult to sink, and reinforcements were on their way.

The sinking of the *Prince of Wales* by Japanese air attack was due, more than any other technical factor, to the lack of consideration given before the war to the problem of shock from near-

misses exploding underwater. It was this shock which knocked out most of the *Prince of Wales'* auxiliary power and thereby deprived her of her hitherto effective anti-aircraft barrage (the 5.25-inch (133-mm) guns were in powered mountings), and, later, of vitally needed pumps. The later ships of the class, *Anson* and *Howe*, were still being built at the time of the *Prince of Wales'* loss, and as a result were fitted with improved damage control arrangements, including auxiliary machinery mounted flexibly to reduce shock damage.

The fact that they were only armed with the 14-inch (356-mm) gun seemed to make little practical difference to the effectiveness of *King George V*'s shooting against *Bismarck*, or *Duke of York*'s against *Scharnhorst*. Because of the piecemeal nature of wartime additions to anti-aircraft armament and radar, not one of the five ships was exactly the same as another, and all changed their appearance slightly during the course of their war service.

The increasing importance of carriers and then aircraft, which by the end of the war had reduced the remaining ships in the *King George V* class to the status of large anti-aircraft escorts and fast bombardment ships for the British Pacific Fleet, also meant that the next class of British battleships were never completed. These were to have been known as the *Lion* class, larger and improved versions of the *King George V* with triple 16-inch (406-mm) turrets.

However, one other battleship was built, specifically designed as a fast battleship with the Pacific in mind, the *Vanguard*. To speed up delivery she used spare 15-inch (380-mm) gun mountings built during the First World War (the story that she was built to take advantage of the availability of these turrets is, however, false). Though these were old guns, they were, as we have seen, excellent, and in every other way the *Vanguard* was a very up-to-date ship. Her raised bow gave her an advantage in seaworthiness over her predecessors; she was also a better sea-boat than the larger American *Missouri* class, which made the American ships' advantage in speed a marginal one. *Vanguard* had probably the best system of battleship protection ever devised. She, rather than *Bismarck*, the clumsy *Yamato*, or the *Iowa*, was probably the best all-round battleship design produced by the war. Alas, she had only one disadvantage: she was completed too late to serve in it.

Howe

HOWE
Displacement 36,830 tons (37,421 tonnes) standard, 40,990 tons (41,648 tonnes) full load
Length 745 feet (227 m)
Beam 103 feet (31 m 39 cm)
Draught 28 feet (8 m 53 cm)
Machinery 4-shaft geared steam turbines, 110,000 shp = $29\frac{1}{4}$ knots
Armour belt: 14 to 15 inches (356 to 380 mm). deck: $2\frac{1}{2}$ to 6 inches (64 to 152 mm). turrets: 9 to 16 inches (227 to 405 mm)
Guns 10 × 14-inch (356-mm), 16 × 5.25-inch (133-mm) DP, 6 × 8-barrelled 40-mm pom-poms
Torpedo Tubes none
Launched 9 April 1940 by Fairfield, Govan

Above: Howe *passing through the Suez Canal in 1944.* Right: Duke of York *steams at speed with the Home Fleet in 1943*

Cruisers

It has always been difficult to find an adequate short definition for the cruiser as a type. Historically the word has covered virtually everything between the huge and powerful armoured cruisers of 1900, as big as battleships, down to small vessels difficult to distinguish from sloops or gunboats. Also there is no clear line of development such as there is in the evolution of the battleship or the destroyer. However, by the end of the First World War there was some degree of order in the types of cruiser in the Royal Navy. The old kind of armoured cruiser was vanishing, though most cruisers had some form of protective plating, usually deck and side armour. There were a number of small fast cruisers designed primarily for the North Sea. By 1939 the earlier surviving examples of these (the 'C' class) had all been converted, or were undergoing conversion, to anti-aircraft ships. Armed with high-angle 4-inch (102-mm) guns they proved very effective in this role. The later class, the 'D' ships, were not heavily rebuilt. but in general used for second-line duties. The exception to the rebuilding rule was the *Delhi*, which was converted in the USA to a main armament of five of the excellent American 5-inch (127-mm) destroyer guns in place of her original 6-inch (152-mm) mounts. This was a trial installation, as the Admiralty was seriously considering the possibility of using this weapon in British destroyers.

The older type of trade-route cruiser was the original 'Town' type, of which only one, the Australian *Adelaide*, survived to serve in the Second War. These were armed with 6-inch (152-mm) guns, as were two fast cruisers still being built at the end of the war, the *Emerald* and *Enterprise*. However, the most influential vessels being built then were a class of larger cruisers armed with 7.5-inch (190-mm) guns, the *Cavendish* class. It was these ships which were responsible for the adoption of 8-inch (203-mm) guns as the maximum calibre for cruisers in the interwar naval treaties, and also the 10,000-ton limitation on tonnage. Other than this, their importance was not great, as they were merely enlarged versions of the smaller cruisers, retaining single gun mounts.

The first post-war ships were very different. These were the 'Counties', the original 'treaty cruisers'. Because of their high freeboard and their archaic-looking triple funnels, and also because of the fact that the British did not cheat on displacement as blatantly as most other naval powers, this large group of ships came to be looked upon as inferior to their foreign contemporaries. However the 'Counties' were to prove excellent fighting ships; their twin 8-inch (203-mm) mounting was a very powerful and effective weapon indeed, their speed and endurance were both adequate to meet most demands, and despite a propensity to roll a lot, they were

good sea-boats. Their protection was also reasonable, the magazines were armoured, and so was half of the machinery space. The last two of the 'Counties' were to have been built with a two-knot drop in speed, traded for an increase in armour thickness and extent. Unfortunately these two interesting ships, the *Northumberland* and *Surrey*, were cancelled.

The 'Counties' were all described as 'A'-class cruisers under the treaty definitions but there was also provision for 8-inch (203-mm) cruisers of the 'B' type, a kind of cheap version. The length and breadth of the 'County' design were reduced, and three as against four 8-inch (203-mm) turrets were fitted. Freeboard was generally reduced, and the flush deck of the 'Counties' was abandoned for a cut-down after deck. Three funnels were replaced by two, though the power of the machinery was not changed.

Only two ships of this kind were built, the *York* and the *Exeter*. The *Exeter* differed from her slightly earlier sister by having a lower bridge and unraked funnels, and she also had two fixed catapults angled outwards abaft the funnels. In all cruisers of this time great importance was given to the aircraft arrangements, which were indeed to prove useful early in the war for isolated cruisers on patrol in the oceans. Later the increasing availability of carrier aircraft lessened the need for the amphibians catapulted

Exeter

from battleships and cruisers.

HMS *Exeter*, like all the 'Counties' and most other British cruisers, had a secondary anti-aircraft armament of high-angle 4-inch (102-mm) guns, and also carried 21-inch (530-mm) torpedo tubes. It was, however, her excellent protection which was probably her greatest asset in her most famous action, against the *Graf Spee*. This enabled her to continue to divert the pocket battleship's fire from *Ajax* and *Achilles* even after virtually all her armament was out of action and she had suffered other heavy damage. She thus played her part to the limit in the carefully planned anti-raider tactics which had been developed by the Admiralty to deal with the pocket battleships before the war. It was definitely not a brilliant improvisation

by the local commander which had the three British cruisers dividing into two forces, for this was a manoeuvre practiced on several occasions before the war by all British cruiser squadrons.

After *Exeter*, Britain built no more cruisers armed with 8-inch (203-mm) guns mainly because it was considered that the rate of fire and ease of handling of 6-inch (152-mm) guns more than compensated for that weapon's lesser range, particularly if the cruiser carrying such guns was armoured to resist 8-inch (203-mm) gunfire. Nevertheless, 8-inch (203-mm) shells fired from 'County'-class cruisers inflicted vital damage on two German capital ships. In the case of the *Bismarck* it was her fire control which was knocked out, while the *Scharnhorst*'s radar was irreparably damaged.

Exeter firing at aircraft, showing her added tripod masts and heavy a/a armament

EXETER
Displacement 8,390 tons (8,524 tonnes) standard, 10,500 tons (10,668 tonnes) full load
Length 575 feet (175 m 25 cm)
Beam 58 feet (17 m 67 cm)
Draught 17 feet (5 m 18 cm)
Machinery 4-shaft geared steam turbines, 80,000 shp = $32\frac{1}{4}$ knots
Armour belt: 2 to 3 inches (51 to 76 mm). deck: 2 inches (51 mm). turrets: $1\frac{1}{2}$ to 2 inches (38 to 51 mm)
Guns 6 × 8-inch (203-mm), 4 × 4-inch (102-mm) AA, 2 × 2-barrelled 40-mm pom-poms
Torpedo Tubes 6 × 21-inch (530-mm)
Launched 18 July 1929 at Devonport Dockyard

Ajax

By 1930 the majority of British 6-inch (152-mm)-gun light cruisers were becoming obsolete, and various other navies were producing modern cruiser designs, such as the German *Königsberg* class, with enclosed gun-houses and other modern refinements. This was the background against which the *Leander* class were designed. There were five, named *Achilles*, *Ajax*, *Leander*, *Neptune* and *Orion*, handsome symmetrical ships with a single trunked funnel. The most important design considerations were an armament of eight 6-inch (152-mm) guns and a speed of 32 knots. The twin mounting with its enclosed gun-house was developed from that fitted in the cruiser *Enterprise* and then the battleships *Nelson* and *Rodney*.

Unlike some of their contemporaries, particularly the Italian 152-mm cruisers, the *Leanders* had a reasonable amount of armour protection, which paid off when *Ajax* and *Achilles* had to take on *Graf Spee*. *Neptune* demonstrated the efficiency of her underwater protection by setting off four mines before sinking in a Mediterranean minefield.

One disadvantage of the *Leander* class, otherwise excellent and well-balanced fighting ships, was that their machinery was not on the unit system; in other words, boiler rooms adjoined one another and could all be knocked out by a single hit. This was rectified in the next design, the 'Modified *Leander*' class with machinery spaces in the sequence of boiler room – engine room – boiler room – engine room. This necessitated a return to two funnels, giving the new class a less massive but perhaps more elegant appearance. All three were transferred to the Royal Australian Navy as the *Hobart*, *Perth* and *Sydney*.

The next class of ships to appear were reduced versions of the previous one. The *Arethusa* class were intended first and foremost for trade protection, and were of the minimum size compatible with seaworthiness. They had an armament of six 6-inch (152-mm) guns, adequate against an armed merchant raider, and a speed of about 32 knots, which was necessary as they

AJAX

Displacement 6,985 tons (7,097 tonnes) standard, 8,950 tons (9,073 tonnes) full load
Length 554 feet 3 inches (168 m 93 cm)
Beam 55 feet 9 inches (16 m 99 cm)
Draught 16 feet (4 m 87 cm)
Machinery 4-shaft geared turbines, 72,000 shp = 32½ knots
Armour belt: 2 to 4 inches (51 to 102 mm). deck: 2 inches (51 mm). turrets: 1 inch (25 mm)
Guns 8 × 6-inch (152-mm), 8 × 4-inch (102-mm) AA, 4 quadruple MGs
Torpedo Tubes 8 × 21-inch (530-mm)
Launched 1 March 1934 by Vickers-Armstrong, Barrow

Ajax after her 1940 refit with tripod masts fitted. The catapult and aircraft have been removed. The prominant knuckle forward was a feature of most British cruisers, but the unusual single trunked funnel led the Graf Spee *to confuse her and her sister* Achilles *with destroyers early in the River Plate action. The fire control carries gunnery radar and the small tower abaft it supports a surface radar search. In common with her surviving sisters she had an X turret replaced by light a/a guns in 1944*

Penelope

were also intended to act as fleet cruisers if required.

They were 50 feet (15.2 m) shorter than the preceeding class, and had only one twin turret aft, but otherwise were very similar, except for their 'chopped off' look aft. They were attractive little ships and an excellent design. They could do anything bigger cruisers could do, but were cheaper and required a smaller crew. It is a pity that Britain did not build more of these instead of the later 'Town' class, impressive ships though the latter undoubtedly were. The *Arethusa* ships' anti-aircraft armament was much the same as their bigger sisters', and the armour protection was only slightly less. One interesting feature was that, for the first time in British ships of this type, welding played an important part in construction in order to save weight.

Ironically this class were mainly employed in fleet work in the confined waters of the Mediterranean, and saw little of the trade routes for which they were designed. *Penelope*, in particular, operating from Malta, had an impressive record and it is she who is immortalized in C S Forester's famous novel *The Ship* as HMS *Artemis*.

Later, when the Admiralty required a small cruiser design primarily intended for anti-aircraft work, the *Arethusa* design was modified to fit. Instead of a main armament of 6-inch (152-mm) guns and a secondary high-angle outfit of 4-inch (102-mm) guns, the new class was given ten dual-purpose 5.25-inch (133-mm) guns in twin mounts. These weapons were perhaps a little heavy for anti-aircraft work, though perfectly adequate if a little complicated as low-angle weapons. The new ship class, the *Dido* vessels, were handicapped by a shortage of mountings and two, the *Scylla* and *Charybdis*, had eight 4.5-inch (114-mm) guns each instead of 5.25-inch (133-mm) weapons. Although they were known as the 'toothless terrors', they were more useful than their sisters for anti-aircraft duties. As ten guns were found to fire off the ammunition rather faster than was prudent a second improved group were given eight guns instead, as well as upright instead of raked funnels. All gave good service in the war, especially in the Mediterranean, and proved the basic soundness of the design and concept of this particular type of light cruiser.

Penelope entering Grand Harbour, Malta probably in 1942 after bomb damage had been repaired at Gibraltar. The artwork depicts this ship before the outbreak of war, except for the tripods. These ships were too small to carry the catapult and aircraft normally considered necessary for cruisers of the Second World War period

PENELOPE
Displacement 5,270 tons (5,342 tonnes) standard, 6,715 tons (6,819 tonnes) full load
Length 506 feet (154 m 22 cm)
Beam 51 feet (15 m 54 cm)
Draught 14 feet (4 m 26 cm)
Machinery 4-shaft geared turbines, 64,000 shp = 32¼ knots
Armour belt: 2 to 2¾ inches (51 to 70 mm). deck: 2 inches (51 mm). turrets: 1 inch (25 mm)
Guns 6 × 6-inch (152-mm), 8 × 4-inch (102-mm) AA, 2 quadruple MGs
Torpedo Tubes 6 × 21-inch (530-mm)
Launched 15 October 1935 by Harland & Wolff, Belfast

From the lighter 6-inch (152-mm) cruisers we now shift to the heavier ones. Japan, with the *Mogami* class, and the United States with the *Brooklyn* class, had both produced very large 6-inch (152-mm) cruisers, fully the equal of the older 8-inch (203-mm) treaty cruisers. Britain followed suit, though in slightly more conservative fashion, as her heavy 6-inch (152-mm) cruisers only had 12 as opposed to 15 guns. Ironically these ships, because of their guns, continued to be known as 'light' cruisers despite their large size.

The British, like their rivals, adopted triple turrets, though with the special feature of having the central gun further back than the two outer weapons, to avoid blast interference problems. The first group of ships built for the Royal Navy with this turret were known by the old 'Town' names, and were called the *Southampton* class. In many ways they were enlarged versions of the *Amphion* or Australian 'Improved *Leander*' class. Armour protection was improved and thickened, and a hangar built on either side of the forefunnel. These were heavy and powerful ships, but towards the end of the war the addition of topweight in the form of radar and extra light guns caused the superimposed turret aft to be removed to preserve the ships' stability. This modification was also applied to the later 'Colony' class, but not to the survivor (*Belfast*) of the two improved 'Towns' which were the largest British cruisers of the war.

These two ships looked quite different from the other 'Towns', as the machinery was moved further aft, the after turrets were mounted higher, and two extra twin 4-inch (102-mm) high-angle mountings added. There was a somewhat unsightly gap between bridge and forefunnel, but these were very powerful ships indeed, having been lengthened and given extra armour protection. Because she broke her back when mined early in the war, *Belfast* was rebuilt with external bulges, which did not add to the beauty of her appearance, and she now survives as a museum ship in London.

The next class ordered after the 'Towns' were the 'Colonies', basically similar to the earlier class except that they were restricted to 8,000 tons (8,130 tonnes) instead of 10,000 tons (10,160 tonnes) because of the London Naval Treaty. Despite this, careful design meant that little of value was lost in the weight saving; the stern was a flat transom instead of the more elegant 'cruiser' stern, mast and funnels were vertical instead of raked, and protection had to be slightly reduced and rearranged. Other than this the first group of the 'Colonies', of which *Jamaica* was one, were similar to the *Southampton* class. The later ships were modified to give better accommodation to radar and light guns, while dispensing from the beginning with 'X' turret, which was also removed from the earlier ships.

The chief disadvantage of the 'Colonies' was

that their reduced tonnage as against the 'Towns' meant that accommodation was cramped, and became more so as the men necessary to work the extra light guns and radar had to be added to their complement. Apart from this, they were excellent, well-balanced fighting ships, very much in the British cruiser tradition. The design was modified only slightly in the next class, the *Swiftsure*, only three of which were completed by the end of the war. Another three were kept for several years in a partly-completed state until they were equipped with new automatic weapons, but these ships, the *Tiger* class, take us far beyond the war period.

JAMAICA

Displacement 8,525 tons (8,661 tonnes) standard, 10,350 tons (10,516 tonnes) full load
Length 555 feet 6 inches (169 m 31 cm)
Beam 62 feet (18 m 89 cm)
Draught 16 feet 6 inches (5 m)
Machinery 4-shaft geared turbines, 72,500 shp = 33 knots
Armour belt: 3¼ inches (82 mm). deck: 2 inches (51 mm). turrets: 2 inches (51 mm)
Guns 12 × 6-inch (152-mm), 8 × 4-inch (102-mm) AA, 2 × 4-barrelled 40-mm pom-poms
Torpedo Tubes 6 × 21-inch (530-mm)
Launched 16 November 1940 by Vickers-Armstrong, Barrow

Top: Jamaica, a 'Colony'-class cruiser, seen off Iceland. Right: Belfast after her rebuild

Jamaica

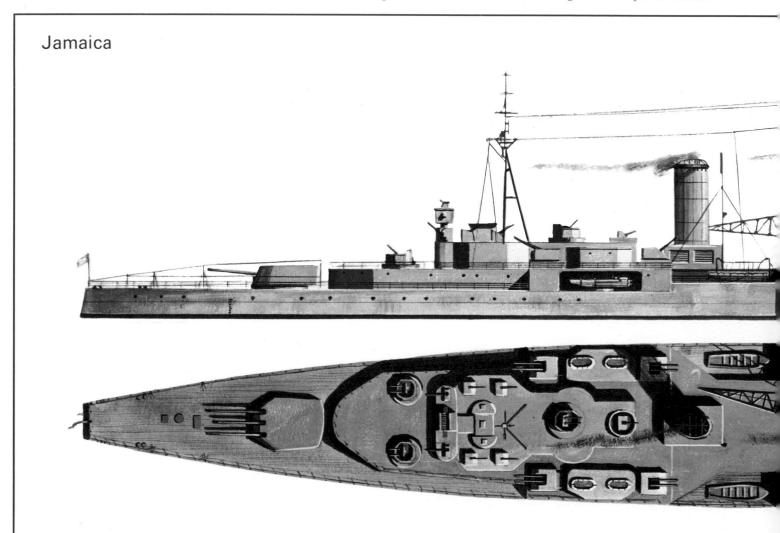

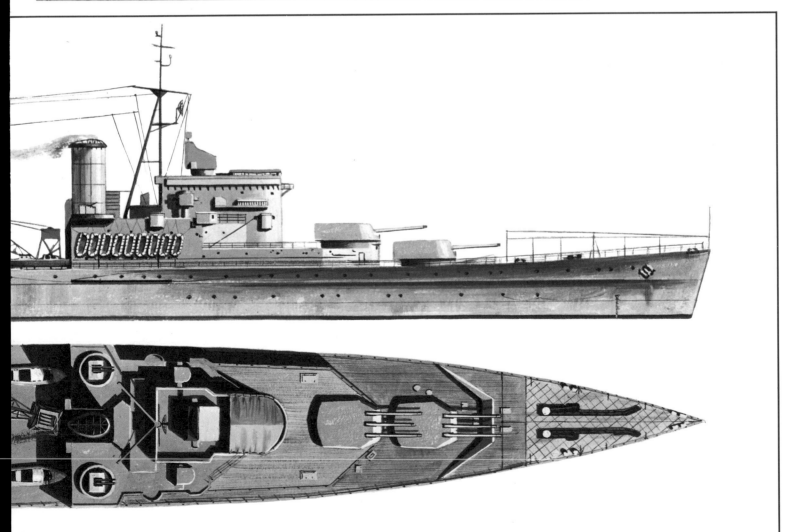

Destroyers

During the First World War the Royal Navy developed what was perhaps the classic destroyer design of all time. Certainly the sturdy 'V & W' class were far and away the best design of their own period; they were equipped with four 4-inch (102-mm) guns (4.7-inch (120-mm) in the later ships of the class) in superimposed mounts, and two multiple torpedo-tubes. They had a good speed, reliable machinery, and were very seaworthy. Many were converted to anti-aircraft ships or long-range escorts, and despite their age they won a great deal of affection from their crews.

The basic formula of the 'V & W' design was copied widely by other navies, and it remained the basis of British destroyer design until just before the Second World War. The 'A' to 'I' classes were all two-funnelled, four-gun vessels (except for the leaders which had five guns) of approximately the same size and performance. They were excellent ships, and they proved to be a match for much larger and better-armed German vessels thanks to their seaworthiness. Their main disadvantage proved to be that they did not have the displacement to accept all the radar and light anti-aircraft guns that the war showed to be necessary for a modern destroyer.

The famous 'Tribal' class were built just before the war because of fears about the increasing size and gunpower of large Japanese, German and French destroyers. They were basically an enlargement of the previous destroyers with twin mountings in place of singles for 4.7-inch (120-mm) guns, and only one set of torpedo tubes. Unfortunately, like the earlier ships, they were deficient in high-angle fire, which was also true of the classes that followed, though stopgaps like replacing one gun or torpedo mounting with an anti-aircraft gun worked reasonably well. The 'Tribals' were in fact probably an uneconomic design; what really mattered in destroyers was numbers, and the next design, the 'J & K' class, gave over twice the number of torpedo tubes with only one less twin 4.7-inch (120-mm) mounting, on a smaller displacement. Weight was saved by using a different system of construction, longitudinal framing, and also by using only two boilers, hence the single funnel that became typical of British destroyers built during the war.

With some alterations in dimensions and the adoption of the simpler and more economical system of having the main armament in four single mounts, the 'J & K' design became the basis of the British standard wartime destroyer design. Towards the end it became apparent that this was no longer large enough, but it was a reliable and sturdy design and did its work well. It was not until the end of the war that the first of the completely new designs began to emerge. These were the large and powerful 'Battle' class, with their main gun armament concentrated forward, and excellent torpedo and light anti-aircraft armament. This class also had better range, being intended primarily for use in the Pacific.

Unlike the Germans and Americans, the British did not go in for high-pressure steam machinery until after the war was over. This was

because of the mishandling of the trials of high-pressure boilers in one of the 'A' class, long before the war; the installation was not given a fair chance to prove itself, so the Royal Navy was saddled with machinery that gave less economy and range than other navies' destroyers. On the other hand this was not all bad, as British machinery was normally very reliable. The Germans' unhappy experience with high-pressure steam machinery demonstrates the dangers of adopting such technical innovations too rapidly.

Top left: The 'K' class destroyer Kashmir *with her famous flotilla leader* Kelly *behind. Above:* Onslow *in December 1942, showing the damage from 203-mm shells during the Barents Sea action. Top right: A sister of the* Onslow, Orwell *was modified for minelaying; the sponson for the mine rails can be seen right aft. Right: The 'Tribal'-class destroyer* Bedouin *in an Icelandic fiord. She is fitted with a twin 4-inch (102-mm) high-angle mounting in 'X' position; the after funnel has been cut down.* Bedouin *was sunk in the Mediterranean in 1942*

Submarines

British submarines of the Second World War were not particularly exciting designs, but, as one might expect, they were reliable and effective craft which achieved excellent results, though at high cost, in difficult conditions, especially in the Mediterranean.

Apart from the remaining examples of two excellent but now outdated First World War classes, the 'H' and the 'L' submarines, the interwar navy produced a number of large overseas patrol submarines, and some mine-layers. The first of the 'S' class, small submarines for work in areas like the Mediterranean, came out in the early 1930s, but modified examples of this successful design continued to be built throughout the war. The first examples of the even smaller 'U' class which appeared later were originally intended as unarmed training boats, but when fitted with torpedoes and a gun proved very useful in the Mediterranean and other confined waters. The 'U' craft and their successors the 'V's were, like the 'S' class, in production throughout the war. The third type upon which wartime production was standardized were the bigger 'T' class for longer-range work. Towards the end of the war it became apparent that the Pacific campaign

Top: The submarines Taku *(foreground),* Una *and* Unrivalled *in Malta Harbour, probably in late 1942. Right: Three British submarines alongside their depot ship. The nearest is* Tudor *of the larger 'T' class, with two external torpedo tubes visible. The centre 'S'-class submarine with search periscope raised has a single torpedo tube aft, and the outermost 'S'-class submarine is the* Stygian

of subsidiary duties such as towing midget submarines and 'human torpedoes', but the most unusual work done was to ferry supplies to Malta. To do this some of the older submarines had part of their batteries removed, but the big minelayers of the *Porpoise* class proved best suited for the job. Their long, clear mine-decks were easily filled with such items as glycol coolant for Spitfires, machine-gun ammunition and cased fuel, as well as food for the starving civilian and military population of the island. Throughout the worst period from mid-1941 to mid-1942 submarines were among the few vessels which dared make the Malta run, so completely did Italian and German aircraft dominate the approaches.

The most important technical innovation in pre-war submarines was the emphasis on a heavy salvo of torpedoes. It was obvious that British submariners would normally be attacking well-defended warships rather than merchant ships, and so prudence dictated an attack from longer range. To compensate for the loss of accuracy it was therefore necessary to fire a bigger spread, and in the 'T' class four extra torpedo-tubes were fitted externally to raise the bow-salvo to an unprecedented *ten* torpedoes. This provision was more than adequate and two of the external tubes were resited in later 'T' boats to fire aft.

British submarines benefited from the Allies' lead in the design of radar. As soon as sets became available, submarines were given air-warning and surface-warning radar to help them avoid the hunters and stalk their prey. Pre-war submarines had virtually no defence against aircraft, and most wartime submarines were fitted with a conning-tower platform for a 20-mm Oerlikon gun to give even a slight chance of shooting down an aircraft. In other respects British submarines were not heavily modified, unlike German and American submarines, but the 'S' and 'T' classes were given a single torpedo tube aft to remedy their lack of astern fire.

When the minelayer *Seal* fell into German hands after her surrender in the Kattegat in 1940 the Germans were most impressed by her comfortable accommodation. But the comfort was relative, and it is interesting to see that air-conditioning was added to the 'S' and 'T' boats later in the war. In the Pacific this single factor improved efficiency to the point that spare crews could be cut by half, because the health and well-being of operational crews was so drastically improved.

Welding was introduced into submarine construction during the war, and by 1945 the hulls of all the newer boats were fully welded. Despite gloomy predictions from the older hands it proved much more robust than rivetting. One of the reasons behind the building of the 'A' class was the need to speed up construction by altering the design of the 'T' hull to make it easier to weld in sections. Instead of producing two different hulls, expediency dictated that the requirement could best be met by using the new methods in a new class of submarine specially designed for the Pacific.

Above: The conning tower of the submarine Seraph, *showing the air-warning radar aerial to the right of the periscope standards and the breach mechanism of the 20-mm anti-aircraft gun. As the 'ship with two captains' she performed several undercover missions*

would need much bigger vessels, faster on the surface and with greater endurance, so the 'A' class was designed, but only the first of these was being commissioned when V-J Day arrived.

It has often been held against British submarines of this period that their maximum designed diving depth was much less than that of their German equivalents. This is true, but what is not so often realized is that their speed of diving was greater, a most important quality for any submarine, particularly the British, whose prey would normally be difficult to find, well protected, and close in to the enemy's coast.

Despite their problems in finding targets British submarines did very well and sank 6 cruisers, 16 destroyers, 35 submarines, 112 minor warships and auxiliaries, and about 500 merchant ships (totalling 1,525,000 gross tons) – a total of 669 vessels. To achieve this cost 78 submarines lost by enemy action. Well over half were sunk in the Mediterranean, where the clear waters made it very hard to avoid detection by aircraft; only 28 were lost in northern waters and only five in the Pacific. In fact the losses exceeded the number of submarines in existence in September 1939 by a wide margin – a rough indication of both the smallness of the British pre-war submarine force and of its enormous expansion.

British submarines were used for a variety

FRANCE

In 1918 France had a second-class navy. During the interwar years the Washington Naval Treaty limitations, lack of money and restricted building facilities kept it small, but by the outbreak of the Second World War, the French Navy was once more a very formidable force. This was due to the high quality of many of its new ships, particularly the modern light cruisers and large destroyers.

Despite occasional anti-British feelings, the most likely enemy in the interwar years was Italy, and later Germany as well. It is therefore not surprising that most French warships were designed particularly to suit conditions in the Mediterranean and the southern part of the North Sea, where speed was of the utmost importance, and long range and seaworthiness were not so significant.

In 1939, the French possessed only one true aircraft carrier, the *Bearn*, whose conversion from an unfinished *Normandie*-class battleship was completed in 1927. Unlike the contemporary British carrier *Eagle*, her conversion was not particularly successful. This and her slow speed kept *Béarn* out of operational employment during the Second World War; instead she was used as an aircraft transport.

French naval aviation concentrated on sea-planes and flying boats, and in 1929, as a result, the 10,160-tonne seaplane tender *Commandant Teste* was launched. However, the need for aircraft carriers was eventually recognized, and in 1938 the 18,280-tonne *Joffre* and *Painlevé* were ordered, each intended to carry 40 aircraft. Only *Joffre* was laid down, and her construction was abandoned in 1940 when only a quarter complete. She was eventually dismantled on her slipway, which was not, perhaps, a complete disaster, since these two carriers would have compared most unfavourably with British, American or Japanese carriers of the same date. Not only was the flight deck extremely small

for the size of ship, but it was also unarmoured. Therefore these two ships would not have had the equivalent British carriers' capacity to survive heavy damage from bombs, nor did they have the ability of the American and Japanese carriers to carry large numbers of aircraft.

Built in quantity by the French, large destroyers (*contre-torpilleurs*) were intended for high-speed sweeps in enemy-controlled waters. They proved invaluable in the Skaggerak and in the North Sea generally early in the war, and in the Mediterranean throughout the conflict. The first group, the *Chacal* class, were begun in 1922, and were armed with a rather unsatisfactory 130-mm gun. The next four classes (each class was of six ships), built between 1927 and 1936, were armed with the much more satisfactory single 138-mm gun, while the last class (of which only the first two, *Mogador* and *Volta*, were built) were armed with a complex and delicate twin 138-mm mount. All these ships were capable of sustained high-speed cruising. All the ships in the last class with single mountings, the *Fantasque*, achieved speeds of over 40 knots, and one of them, *Le Terrible*, averaged 45.03 knots for eight hours. Although superb vessels in their own setting, they were not suited for oceanic warfare. In the Pacific in particular,

This pre-war photograph of the heavy cruiser Algérie probably shows her running trials in 1934. It would appear that the catapult has not yet been fitted, nor has the secondary armament been mounted. The tower abaft the funnel with its cranes is an unusual feature. The heavy crane forward is for aircraft, while the after crane, smaller and lighter, is for boats. In 1940–41 the tripod mainmast was replaced by a large deck-house carrying light anti-aircraft guns. Obviously the funnel cap seen in this photograph did not succeed in keeping funnel gases away from the bridge, since it was later replaced by a much larger cap

their very short range was an immense handicap. Only a navy that could ignore, or did not have, distant commitments, could afford to build large numbers of such specialized ships. Only the Germans and the Italians copied them in large numbers, and of the Italian equivalents, the 'Capitani Romani' class, only three were ever completed. Instead, the other navies all built numbers of slightly larger and slower light cruisers, which had superior endurance, seaworthiness, and ability to survive battle damage, combined with a steadier gun platform for much the same armament. These light cruisers could be used for a much wider range of functions.

Between 1923 and 1931 the French built 26 destroyers of the very similar *Bourrasque* and *L'Adroit* classes. Like their early interwar cruisers, these were very unexceptional ships, with a disappointingly short range and a not very effective gun.

It was agreed at London in 1930 that any number of small torpedo craft or escorts could be built, as long as they did not exceed 600 tonnes. This was the origin of the *Melpoméne* class, and the Germans and Italians also built numbers of this type of vessel. They were fast and manoeuverable, and were very useful in the confined waters of the Channel and the Mediterranean, but they were really too small. They lacked stability, were poor sea boats and were rather lightly built. In addition, their usefulness in anti-submarine work was considerably diminished by their lack of Asdic. Their shortcomings were soon realized, and after the treaty limitations had been lifted a much bigger design was prepared. The 1,020-tonne *Le Fier* ships were to have had a completely anti-aircraft-gun armament, and if they had been completed would have been a great improvement on the *Melpoméne* vessels.

Meanwhile it had been realized that the *Bourrasque* and *L'Adroit* types were too slow to act as escorts for the new capital ships. A new design, the *Le Hardi* class, was therefore prepared, with a continuous sea speed of 37 instead of 30 knots. In all, 15 were authorized between 1932 and 1940. This was an excellent design, comparing favourably with the best foreign equivalents, its sole weakness being, once again, an unsatisfactory gun mounting. However, French production methods were as slow as usual; it was two years before the design was finally approved, and the first vessels were not laid down until 1934. Only six were completed in time to see service.

At the outbreak of war, the French had a large and efficient fleet of 77 submarines in service, with 24 under construction and 20 more on order. This was not surprising, since France was one of the first countries to produce successful submersibles.

There were three main types of French interwar submarines. The first was the ocean-going submarine. Its primary function was to provide a scouting force and a shield for the fleet, and the emphasis, therefore, was on high surface speed. The nine vessels in the first, or *Requin*, class were 500 tonnes smaller than the succeeding 29 *Redoutable*-class submarines, which were built between 1925 and 1939. Detailed improvements were made to the *Redoubtable* class as time went by, and the later vessels had a surface speed of 21 rather than 19 knots, but the basic design remained the same. The last member of the class, the *Sidi Feruch*, was laid down in 1931, but was not completed until 1939.

Their intended replacements, the *Roland Morillot* class, were authorized in 1934, but the first, the *Roland Morillot* itself, was not laid down until 1937. She was scuttled in 1940 on the day before she was due to be launched. No other member of this class was completed.

The second type was the *Saphir* class of submarine mine-layers, of which the most famous was the *Rubis*. This very successful class of six submarines were built between 1925 and 1937. Both types were designed by the French Admiralty.

The first 26 French interwar coastal submarines were designed by their builders to the same general specification, and it was not until 1930

The submarine Casabianca, *the only French warship which managed to escape and join the allies after the scuttling of the French fleet at Toulon in November 1942, arrives at Algiers. She played an important part in the capture of Corsica*

that the French Admiralty introduced their own standard design, the *Minerve*. In 1935 the first of an enlarged version, the *Aurore* class, was laid down; none of them were completed until after the war. An improved version for tropical service, the *Phénix* class, was authorised, but none were laid down.

The one exception to the above types was the commerce-raiding submarine *Surcouf*. Twice the displacement of any other French submarine, she was the largest in the world until the Japanese I-400s. *Surcouf* was armed with two 203-mm guns, as well as two different sizes of torpedo for warships and merchant vessels, and carried a tiny Besson MB 411 seaplane in a hangar behind the conning tower for reconnaissance. She had been laid down in 1927, when many countries were weighing the advantages of large, heavily armed submarines for raiding, but she was unnecessarily large and complicated for the job. After an eventful wartime career, *Surcouf* was accidentally rammed and sunk by an American merchant ship in 1942.

Apart from some problems with guns and mountings, most of the modern French warships were excellent designs. In the small amount of action the French Navy saw it acquitted itself well. It was defeat on land, and the subsequent destruction, scuttling or disablement of most of the French fleet, that prevented the French ships from showing their worth, not any inherent failure in the ships themselves. The lack of aircraft carriers and the inordinate length of time taken to build the ships would have been of major importance if France had been able to beat back the German invasion. As things turned out, these failings became irrelevant because of the defeat of the French Army.

Capital Ships

Although the French reconstructed all their old battleships to a greater or lesser extent between the wars, they did not indulge in complete remodelling like the Italians and the Japanese. Instead, they preferred to spend their limited money on new ships. As a result, the old ships lacked both the speed and the armour protection necessary for modern warfare. The side armour was particularly thin and both *Provence* and *Bretagne* succumed rapidly to hits by British 15-inch (380-mm) shells during the bombardment of Mers-el-Kebir. Of the five active units of the *Courbet* and *Bretagne* class at the start of the war, only the most extensively converted ship, the *Lorraine*, saw extensive service at both the beginning and end of the war. The *Provence*, salvaged from Mers-el-Kebir, was scuttled at Toulon, and the slightly older *Courbet* and *Paris* were no longer of any operational value by 1944.

The first new French capital ships were the battlecruisers *Dunkerque* and *Strasbourg*. The germ of their design lay in proposals in 1926 for a ship of 17,700 tonnes, with eight 240-mm guns, a speed of not less than 34 knots, with armour sufficient to withstand 8-inch (203-mm) shell hits. The final design, authorized in 1931, was of 26,900 tonnes, with an armament of eight 330-mm guns, a maximum speed of nearly 30 knots, and armour capable of resisting 11-inch (280-mm) shells at normal battle ranges. High speed had given way to heavier guns and greater protection, because the *Dunkerque* and *Strasbourg*, in addition to acting as commerce raiders and fleet scouts, were intended to cope not only with 10,160-tonne cruisers, as were the previous proposed designs drawn up by the French in the late 1920s, but also with the 'pocket battleships'.

The most unusual feature of these ships was the placing of the main armament in two four-gun turrets forward, and the dual-purpose secondary armament in three four-gun and two twin turrets aft. This was based on the arrangement in HMS *Nelson*, and had the same advantage of reducing the length, and therefore the weight, of the armour belt (even though the turrets were far apart to avoid both being disabled by one lucky hit), but using two four-gun turrets for the main armament instead of three triple turrets to allow for the greatest number of heavy guns on the smallest possible displacement. The French had intended using similar four-gun turrets in their *Normandie*- and *Lyon*-class battleships, but of these, only the *Béarn* was completed, and then as an aircraft carrier, not as a battleship. Theoretically, the dead arc astern in the *Dunkerque* and *Strasbourg* was only 23° on each side, but in practice, as with all ships with their armament concentrated forward, the blast from the heavy guns was so severe that they were rarely fired abaft the beam.

The use of four- as well as two-gun turrets for the secondary armament (unlike the six twin-turret arrangement of the *Nelson*) was a failure. The four-gun turrets were too unwieldy, and the loading mechanism too fragile, particularly for anti-aircraft work. The secondary armament was the weakest point in the whole design.

Although the side armour was very thin for a modern capital ship, it was adequate for its designed function and was sloped to give the maximum possible protection, while the horizontal armour was satisfactory. The underwater protection was good. Despite their light construction and armour, these ships were capable of surviving considerable punishment, as *Dunkerque* demonstrated at Mers-el-Kebir.

A major flaw was the inadequate range, which was revealed early in the war during the pursuit of German surface raiders in the Atlantic. However, on balance the *Dunkerque* was a successful design. The ships were capable of fulfilling their designed tasks and comparing very favourably with their somewhat larger and slightly later German equivalents *Scharnhorst* and *Gneisenau*, and were almost certainly a match for their Italian counterparts, the much reconstructed *Cavour* and *Duilio* classes. It is interesting that the American *Alaska* class, designed to fulfil a very similar function, had almost identical thicknesses of armour.

One of the ironies of war is that the only action the *Dunkerque* ships fought was against battleships, under conditions where it was only by a combination of luck and good management that one of them, *Strasbourg*, was able to use her superior speed. As in all pre-1939 French warships, great emphasis was placed on speed; the French Navy was acutely aware of the Italian warships' reputed performance. On her trials the *Dunkerque* steamed for eight hours at 30.57 knots with her Parsons single-reduction turbines developing 114,000 horsepower, and for two hours maintained 31 knots with 135,585 horsepower. Her sister ship *Strasbourg* did equally well, and both ships steamed economically at 20 knots.

An American soldier stands on the forecastle of the French battle-cruiser Strasbourg. *She was scuttled at Toulon in 1942, salvaged by the Italian Navy, sunk by Allied bombing and eventually raised again. The 330-mm guns in the fore turret have been cut off, presumably for salvage*

Dunkerque

DUNKERQUE

Displacement 30,750 tons (31,243 tonnes) normal, 35,500 tons (36,069 tonnes) full load
Length 703 feet 9 inches (214 m 50 cm)
Beam 102 feet 3 inches (31 m 18 cm)
Draught 28 feet 9 inches (8 m 76 cm)
Machinery 4-shaft geared steam turbines, 112,500 shp = 29½ knots
Armour belt: 5¾ to 9¾ inches (145 to 245 mm). deck: 2 to 5½ inches (51 to 136 mm). turrets: 10 to 13 inches (254 to 330 mm)
Guns 8 × 13-inch (330-mm), 16 × 5.1-inch (130-mm) DP, 8 × 37-mm AA
Aircraft 4 (1 catapult)
Launched 24 December 1932 by Brest Naval Yard

Left: The wide separation of the battle-cruiser Dunkerque's *quadruple main turrets is clearly visible, with the large hangar aft, immediately in front of the catapult. Above: This fine action shot was taken at Mers-el-Kebir on 3 July 1940. In the foreground, the still-undamaged* Provence *trains her 340-mm gun turrets to starboard to provide covering fire while her sister ship* Bretagne *blazes in the background, mortally hit by British 15-inch (380-mm) shells. The* Strasbourg *can be seen getting up steam for her breakout*

The guns were a new calibre, 330-mm in place of the older 339-mm. At the maximum elevation of 35° the guns could range out to 32.7 km, and a well-trained crew could fire three rounds per minute. Another interesting feature of the armament was the provision of two different marks of 130-mm guns, one for low-angle work and another with a lighter shell for high-angle (anti-aircraft) firing. It was a partial step towards the idea of a dual-purpose armament well ahead of other navies, but the high-angle mounting was not well designed. The anti-aircraft guns were sited aft, while the low-angle weapons were level with the forward superstructure, which would have provided the heaviest anti-aircraft fire in the right area.

As in the Italian battleships the aircraft catapult was carried on the quarterdeck, but a large hangar was provided to house the four Loire-Nieuport 130 seaplanes. These twin-engined aircraft were very large for shipboard use, regardless of their value in long-range reconnaissance.

The main recognition feature was the massive tower bridge, which was another idea copied from the British *Nelson*. It was even large enough to accommodate a lift for internal communication. The ships were handsome and well proportioned, with the two massive turrets forward balanced by the heavy secondary battery aft. The *Strasbourg* could be distinguished by having a two-storied lower bridge and other minor differences in her control tower.

The *Dunkerque* was badly hit by shells from the *Hood* at Mers-el-Kebir in July 1940, and had to stop firing when she lost electrical power. A day later she was even more badly damaged when a British aerial torpedo exploded depth-charges in a patrol vessel lying alongside. After lengthy repairs she reached Toulon in 1942, only to be scuttled when German troops tried to capture Toulon Dockyard. The *Strasbourg* was luckier at Mers-el-Kebir, but she too had to be scuttled at Toulon in November 1942. While Italian engineers were working on her in 1944 she was sunk again by Allied bombing.

The first new French battleships, the *Richelieu* class, were authorized in 1935, and were basically enlarged versions of the *Dunkerque*, with 380-mm guns and battleship protection. The major armament was in two four-gun turrets forward, and the dual-purpose secondary armament was in three triple turrets aft. Originally *Richelieu* and *Jean Bart* were to have had the same profile as *Dunkerque*, but the funnel shape was drastically remodelled to avoid smoke blowing over the conning tower.

The third member of the class, *Clemenceau*, which was never completed, was to have been slightly different, with more secondary armament and no aircraft or catapult. The fourth, *Gascogne*, and two more projected to follow, were to have been different again. Instead of having both main turrets forward they were to have had one quadruple 380-mm turret forward and the other aft, with two secondary turrets superfiring forward and one superfiring aft.

In the event, only *Richelieu* was completed to more or less the original plan. Laid down in 1935, she was running preliminary sea trials when the Germans invaded France. *Jean Bart* was not laid down until 1939, and barely escaped capture by the Germans in 1940; she left France with only her fore turret mounted and only half her machinery working. *Clemenceau* was also laid down in 1939, but her hull was never completed.

Richelieu was built in a dry dock at Brest naval yard, and *Clemenceau* was begun on the same day that *Richelieu* was launched. *Jean Bart* was built in special jigs at St Nazaire, and *Gascogne* was intended to be built in these too. It was originally intended that these four ships should operate as two groups of two, but when two further battleships were authorized in April 1940, to the same plan as *Gascogne*, it was intended that they should operate as two groups of three, each group containing ships with the same arrangement of main armament.

Jean Bart was not finally completed until 1946 and she was fitted with a completely different bridge structure and a much heavier anti-aircraft armament than that fitted to *Richelieu*. She also had a bulge fitted along half her length to counteract the weight of additional armament and radar. The main armament was the heaviest yet seen in the French Navy. The 380-mm gun fired a 880 kg shell a distance of

32 km at maximum 35° elevation. It had a high velocity by comparison with the British and German weapons of the same calibre, which indicates that it was probably not as accurate at long range. The problems encountered with the quadruple dual-purpose mounting in the *Dunkerque* class resulted in a change to a new triple 152-mm turret. Very little is known about this weapon apart from the fact that its range was 19.75 km.

The machinery was very similar to that of the *Dunkerque*, four-shaft Parsons single-reduction turbines using steam at 35°C from six Indret-Sural boilers. The designed power was 150,000 shaft horsepower, but the *Richelieu* was claimed to have reached 32.5 knots with 179,000 shp in service. When her sister ship *Jean Bart* finally ran her trials in 1949 she reached 31.84 knots with 162,855 shp over six hours; the maximum speed for two hours was 32 knots with 176,000 shp. As this ship displaced about 2,540 tonnes more than the *Richelieu* and had been fitted with bulges to compensate for added topweight the unofficial figure given for the *Richelieu* is probably correct.

The *Richelieu* saw more active service than most French major warships. After her escape to Dakar she helped to repel the British and Free French assault on that port in September 1940, and in 1942 she joined the Allies. To refit a French warship, in which even screw-threads were different, was quite beyond the resources of the hard-pressed British dockyards, and so the *Richelieu* went to the United States in 1943. Largely as a gesture of Allied solidarity, the US Navy undertook the mammoth task of repairing the ravages of war and bringing the battleship up to date. The aircraft and catapults were removed and the anti-aircraft armament was entirely replaced by standard Allied 40-mm and 20-mm weapons. The opportunity was taken to improve her endurance by increasing her fuel stowage by 500 tonnes.

The *Richelieu* bore a distinct family

resemblance to the *Dunkerque* but lacked the elegance of the older ship. Although she had a long, flared forecastle and the same balance of heavy guns forward and secondary turrets aft, her superstructure was a mass of small range-finders and controls. In place of the capped funnel of the *Dunkerque*, the funnel was incorporated into the after control tower and projected at an ugly angle.

Because their only actions against heavy units were as floating batteries while incomplete, it is difficult to judge the worth of the *Richelieu* class. Technically, they compare very well with their contemporaries, including their prospective enemies, the *Bismarck* and *Littorio* classes. Their main drawback for oceanic warfare was their short range, though this was greater than that of the *Littorio* vessels.

France's failure with battleships lay not in their design but in the leisurely rate of peacetime construction, which, combined with the policy of using her very limited resources to reconstruct her old battleships only partially, and to concentrate on building new ships, meant that when war was declared, France did not have any first-class battleships.

RICHELIEU
Displacement 43,293 tons (43,923 tonnes) normal, 47,548 tons (48,311 tonnes) full load
Length 813 feet 3 inches (247 m 89 cm)
Beam 108 feet 3 inches (33 m)
Draught 31 feet 9 inches (9 m 67 cm)
Machinery 4-shaft geared steam turbines, 150,000 shp = 30 knots
Armour belt: $13\frac{1}{2}$ inches (342 mm). deck: 2 to $6\frac{3}{4}$ inches (51 to 170 mm). turrets: $10\frac{1}{2}$ to $17\frac{1}{2}$ inches (266 to 417 mm)
Guns 8 × 15-inch (380-mm), 9 × 6-inch (152-mm) DP, 12 × 3.9-inch (100 mm) AA, 16 × 37-mm AA
Launched 17 January 1939 by Brest Naval Yard

Above right: Richelieu *in 1944–45, with the British Eastern Fleet. Below right:* Richelieu's *guns open up at Sabang*

Richelieu

Cruisers

The early French interwar cruisers were unexceptional vessels. The *Duguay Trouin*-class light cruisers were fast and reliable, and the first of the 10,160-tonne 203-mm cruisers, the *Duquesne* class, were little more than enlarged versions, but both classes had very little protection. The *Suffren* class of 10,160-tonne cruisers were improved vessels of the *Duquesne* class and each of the four *Suffren* ships had improvements in its protection. In the first, *Suffren*, laid down in 1926, the protection weighed 967 tonnes, while in the last, the *Dupleix*, laid down in 1929, the weight of protection was almost doubled to 1,575 tonnes. All these classes suffered from very restricted endurance and the *Duquesne* and the *Suffren* vessels were certainly not the equal of their foreign contemporaries as all-round fighting ships.

In complete contrast, the last French 10,160-tonne cruiser, *Algérie*, was probably the best of her size in the world. Excellently protected, with an adequate range and a powerful anti-aircraft armament, her improved hull design gave only slightly less smooth-water speed with considerably less power than the *Suffren* class. It was not until after the Treaty tonnage restrictions were officially lifted after 1935 that appreciably superior heavy cruisers were built by other countries.

Two special-purpose cruisers were completed in 1931: *Pluton* (later renamed *La Tour D'Auvergne*), a minelaying cruiser with a capacity of 290 mines, and the training cruiser *Jeanne D'Arc*. An improved minelaying cruiser, *Emile Bertin*, was completed in 1934, and from this design were developed the *La Galissonniere*-class cruisers, the most successful French cruiser class – fast, well protected and highly seaworthy. The only problem was that each took four years or more to build, whereas their British contemporaries were only taking from one to two years to complete. Thus although the first *La Galissonnière* was laid down in 1931, and the last in 1933, the last ship of the class of six was not completed until the end of 1937, and the first of their slightly improved successors, *De Grasse*, was not laid down until 1938. She was still on the slipway when the Germans invaded, and her sister ships were never laid down. *De Grasse* was completed as an anti-aircraft cruiser to an altered design after the war.

The aircraft arrangements in the *Algérie* were more elaborate than in previous cruisers, with three Loire-Nieuport 130 seaplanes and two catapults carried amidships. After the fall of France in 1940 the catapults were removed to make room for additional anti-aircraft guns. This alteration increased her resemblance to the *Dunkerque* class, for she had a similar tower bridge and capped funnel, with a smaller superstructure aft. As further compensation for the extra weight the tripod mainmast was removed.

Of all the heavy cruisers built under the Washington Treaty limit of 10,000 tons (10,160 tonnes) standard the *Algérie* had the most impressive protection. Accounting for nearly 24 per cent of her normal displacement of 11,270 tonnes (a high percentage by cruiser standards) the armour belt was 108 mm thick over the boilers and machinery, and an internal torpedo bulkhead ran from the forward 203-mm turret to the after one. There was also a 26-mm to 79-mm-thick deck protecting the machinery spaces and magazines. The French were the only front-line navy to retain coal as a form of protection, and the *Algérie* had coal bunkers

ALGERIE

Displacement 11,100 tons (11,278 tonnes) normal, 13,900 tons (14,123 tonnes) full load
Length 610 feet 9 inches (186 m 15 cm)
Beam 65 feet 9 inches (20 m)
Draught 20 feet 3 inches (6 m 18 cm)
Machinery 4-shaft geared steam turbines, 84,000 shp = 31 knots
Armour belt: $4\frac{1}{4}$ inches (108 mm). deck: $1\frac{1}{8}$ to $3\frac{1}{8}$ inches (28 to 79 mm). turrets: $2\frac{3}{4}$ to $3\frac{7}{8}$ inches (70 to 99 mm)
Guns 8 × 8-inch (203-mm), 12 × 3.9-inch (100-mm) AA, 8 × 37-mm AA
Torpedo Tubes 6 × 21.7-inch (547-mm)
Aircraft 2 (2 catapults)
Launched 21 May 1932 by Brest Dockyard

French heavy cruisers parade in line ahead for inspection at a naval review before the outbreak of war

Algérie

between the side armour and the torpedo bulkhead to cushion the effect of torpedo hits. This feature had been discarded by other navies much earlier because it had been demonstrated that the weight saved could be better used in armour, and because tests had shown that a water- or oil-filled compartment also had a damping effect on hits. But of course the need to extend the ships' range was the deciding factor for the French cruisers of this period.

The machinery on the *Algérie* was the most successful aspect of her design for the Rateau-Bretagne turbine was establishing a fine reputation for power and reliability. She exceeded 30 knots with only 75 per cent of her designed power (66,000 shp as against 84,000) and on her full-power trial she reached 31.71 knots with 85,190 shp for six hours, despite displacing 12,200 tonnes. The six Indret boilers had a maximum pressure of 27 kg/cm² and a temperature of 325°C; five were the direct-flue type and one was return-flue. Only in the matter of fuel consumption did the machinery prove disappointing, for in spite of a designed cruising radius of 8,700 miles (13,920 km), (nearly twice that of the *Suffren* class) her actual radius was a mere 5,500 miles (8,800 km) at 15 knots.

In October 1939 the *Algérie* operated with the battle-cruiser *Strasbourg* and the cruiser *Dupleix* in the massive hunt for the *Graf Spee* in the Atlantic. She also took part in the French Navy's gesture of defiance against Italy in June 1940 when Genoa was bombarded, but she returned to base in accordance with the terms of Marshal Petain's armistice with Germany. In November 1940 she escorted the damaged battleship *Provence* from Mers-el-Kebir to Toulon and was then laid up for a lengthy refit. During this time her aircraft installation was removed, and a large structure was built in place of the mainmast to accommodate four four-barrelled 37-mm anti-aircraft mountings, four quadruple 13.2-mm Hotchkiss machine-gun mountings and four single Browning machine-guns.

It is not generally realised that even during the twilight period of the Vichy government the French armed forces pursued advanced research. Scientists had been working on radar since 1934, and air-warning sets existed in 1939. A metric set was installed in the *Richelieu* at Dakar, and an improved set of this type was fitted in the *Algérie* in the spring of 1942. What was even more remarkable was the fact that the Germans did not capture any equipment intact in June 1940. The scuttling of the *Algérie* and the other ships of the Toulon fleet in November 1942 put an end to these experiments.

As a reply to the Italian *Zara* class the *Algérie* was an outstanding cruiser which would have given a good account of herself in the Mediterranean. But the real role for the heavy cruiser was in ocean warfare. Whereas cruisers armed with 150-mm guns proved more than adequate for Mediterranean operations, in the Atlantic the poor endurance of the *Algérie* was a handicap. Three improved *Algérie* vessels were planned, but as their installed power was to be nearly 50 per cent higher it is almost certain that the French Navy was not interested in curing that fault. History has a habit of making nonsense of plans to match individual ships against their foreign competitors; in the long run, the most successful warships are those which perform well in situations which are not foreseen.

The light cruiser Montcalm, *a participant at D-Day, seen at the end of the war*

THE UNITED STATES

For some reason American warships have never received their fair share of attention. The brilliant but flawed German designs, the extraordinary and original Japanese ships, even the classically austere British warships all seem to enjoy a better press. This may be because the Americans, like the British, tended to concentrate on well-balanced, battleworthy designs rather than spectacular ones which exaggerated one quality above others. Perhaps also the aesthetic aspect has had some weight; some American ships of the Second World War period have a certain air of plastic anonymity and give a slight impression of being various components disposed upon a hull, rather than a ship designed as a whole. Be that as it may, American designs certainly proved that they were not inferior to anyone else's in the hard test of war.

American designers, unlike European ones but like their Japanese opposite numbers, had to stress the importance of range in their ships. These ships would have to operate across the immense spaces of the Pacific, or, perhaps, cross the Atlantic to fight. Another result of this was that the Americans paid close attention to the 'fleet train'. Unlike the British who had widely scattered bases on which they thought they could fall back for fuel and repairs, the Americans reckoned on transporting refuelling and maintenance facilities with the fleet in an assemblage of purpose-built auxiliary ships. It was this fleet train which made victory possible in the greatest oceanic campaign of all time, the American battle with Japan in the Pacific.

America had one enormous advantage over all other nations in this war – her shipbuilding potential. Britain was the only country which could begin to approach the United States in this respect, and this was because Britain had the largest and oldest-established shipbuilding industry in the world. But at the same time this meant that British shipbuilding was in many respects old-fashioned, limited in its ability to make major changes, and hampered by possessing too much obsolescent machinery. In 1939 America's shipbuilding strength was, in contrast, more potential than actual. There was a good-

South Dakota (BB-57) *in September 1943, showing the compact superstructure*

sized warship-building capacity, but American yards had built few merchantmen for over two decades. It is significant that the Liberty ship design was only slightly modified from that of a ship built by a British yard (Doxford's). However, America had the industrial capacity, energy and skill to build large shipyards where none had existed before, and to produce vast numbers of a selection of carefully chosen standard designs. Warships and merchantmen came from these new yards in such profusion as to make the US Navy unchallengeably the largest in the world, and also to equip most of the other Allies' navies as well.

The shipbuilding effort was matched by an equally energetic ship repair programme. The battleships hit by the Japanese at Pearl Harbor were completely rebuilt, damaged British warships like the *Illustrious* repaired, French ships such as the *Richelieu* refitted, and so on. Even before America came into the war Britain was heavily dependent on her shipbuilding resources. In return Britain gave freely of her hard-won experience, and the combination of British ideas with American detailed design and production know-how produced such excellent classes as the destroyer escort, the landing ship tank, and escort carrier, and a wide variety of landing craft, coastal craft and others.

It is perhaps appropriate that the most impres-

Above: An Essex-*class carrier. Right: An* Independence-*class light fleet carrier leads an* Essex-*class carrier and battleships*

sive total of submarines sunk by one ship was achieved by the USS *England* in the Pacific. She was an American destroyer escort built to a British requirement and concept, but to an American design, in an American yard. Though the submarines sunk were Japanese, six of them in 12 days, the weapons used, 'Sonar' (the American adaptation of the British 'Asdic') and the 'Hedgehog' ahead-throwing weapon and depth-charge salvoes, had been developed for use by British ships against German U-boats.

Aircraft Carriers

Thanks to the work of a few dedicated air-minded senior officers the US Navy entered the Second World War with a naval air arm which was second to none. The Japanese had more immediate advantages in their operational experience obtained over China, and in their superlative carrier fighter, the 'Zero'. The Americans, however, were basically stronger, for not only did they have enormous technical and manufacturing resources, they also were ahead of anyone else in the techniques of operating aircraft from carriers. Most of their carrier aircraft types in service in 1941, like the Wildcat and Dauntless, were sound designs, capable with intelligent planning and experience of holding their own against Japanese types. As the war went on the enormous energy, skill and resources of the American aircraft industry meant that planes superior to anything the Japanese could produce at speed or in significant numbers were rushed into service, particularly the Hellcat, Avenger and Corsair. More important still, the Japanese could never replace the

skilled pilots they lost, while the American aircrew-training programme was superbly organized and ever-growing.

While the British tended to regard the design of carriers rather in the light of producing a good ship which also carried aircraft as an incidental, the Americans subordinated everything in their designs to carrying the maximum number of aircraft and getting as many of them in the air as possible as quickly as could be managed. For the British the 'ship' qualities of the carriers took first place; for the Americans it was the aircraft-operating qualities that mattered. Thus it was that the American carriers were often less well protected and designed with less attention to their defensive armament. Both approaches were, of course, valid, particularly given the different strategic, technical and tactical factors affecting each navy. It is interesting, however, as we have already seen in the British carriers, that both nations, as the war went on, tended to adopt more and more of their ally's ideas and methods. One thing that the Americans were certainly

right on was in thinking of the carrier's fighters as being their chief defence against aerial attack. However, with their own excellent fighters they could afford to think this way, particularly after radar had been adapted, with a typically American ability to develop an invention to its full extent, to serving the needs of a carrier force.

The superior nature of American carrier aircraft, their sturdiness and ability to land at higher speeds and steeper angles, also meant that American designers did not need to give much attention to eliminating turbulence in the air over their flight decks. A wartime British report wonderingly remarks that it was almost true to say that American carriers were designed in complete defiance of the science of aerodynamics!

The earliest American carrier was the *Langley*, a converted large fast collier which had an experimental installation for the turbo-electric propulsion later fitted to a number of battleships. She was not a particularly useful vessel, and had been relegated to the task of being an aircraft transport before the war broke out.

Lexington

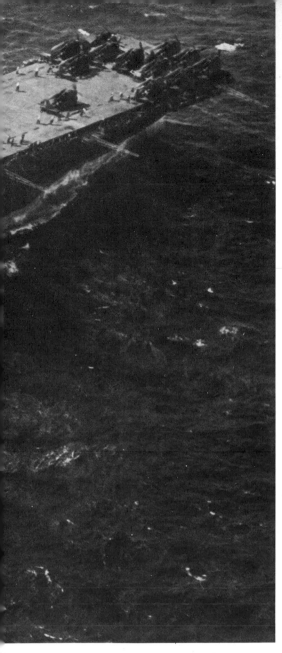

The next two American carriers were very different, and far more effective vessels. It was decided to convert the incomplete hulls of two of the turbo-electric battle-cruisers cancelled as a result of the Washington Naval Treaty to carriers. This was a sensible decision, and the Americans obtained two very large, very fast, and quite well-protected carriers, probably the best of the first generation of this type of ship. Their success makes one wonder whether the British would not have been well advised to have converted the *Hood* to a carrier rather than the job lot of light battle-cruisers and ex-battleships they actually used.

Not every feature of the redesigned *Lexington* and *Saratoga* was justifiable. They were given four twin 8-inch (203-mm) turrets disposed before and abaft the island, a pointless addition as aircraft carriers were far too vulnerable to attempt to 'slug it out' with other warships. These guns were finally removed early in the war, and twin 5-inch (127-mm) turrets substituted. It is sometimes said that *Lexington* was sunk before this could be done to her, but photographs showing her sinking after the Battle of the Coral Sea clearly show the 5-inch (127-mm) mounts.

Gun turrets and the island itself were dwarfed by the most distinctive feature of these ships, a truly enormous funnel. Unlike many later US carriers the bow and the hull were plated up to the level of the flight deck. The plated-in bow was finally readopted by the Americans at the end of the war, but chiefly as a result of the British example.

Because these carriers were not designed as such they could not carry as many planes as they might have done. Even so they managed the impressive total of 90 each. Though the *Lexington* was lost early in the war, the *Saratoga* continued her distinguished career until the end. However, these ships' most important contribution to victory was probably their use in training and exercises in the interwar years, and here their large size and aircraft complement were most important. Smaller ships and fewer aircraft might have meant less satisfactory exercises, less chance to experiment, and less flexibility in trying out new methods.

The first American carrier designed and built as such was the *Ranger*, and in her the American obsession with aircraft capacity was taken to extreme lengths. She only displaced 14,500 tons (14,730 tonnes) when fully laden, yet could carry 86 aircraft, a far greater number than foreign carriers of comparable size, like *Hermes*. Protection, gun armament and speed were adequate but no more, and because of this *Ranger* was usually used for second-line duties during the war. Like most of the later American carriers the hull was not built up to the flight deck. She had the unusual feature of the boiler room being aft of the engine room, and the smoke was emitted through three hinged funnels on each side.

LEXINGTON

Displacement 36,000 tons (36,577 tonnes) standard, 39,000 tons (39,626 tonnes) full load
Length 888 feet (270 m 66 cm)
Beam 130 feet (39 m 62 cm) over flight deck
Draught 24 feet 3 inches (7 m 39 cm)
Machinery 4-shaft steam turbines and electric motors, 184,000 shp = 33¼ knots
Armour belt: 6 inches (152 mm). deck: 1 to 3 inches (25 to 76 mm). turrets 1½ to 3 inches (38 to 76 mm)
Guns 12 × 5-inch (127-mm) AA, 5 × 4-barrelled 1.1-inch (28-mm) AA mountings
Torpedo Tubes none
Aircraft 90 (1 catapult)
Launched 3 October 1925 by Fore River Co., Quincy, Massachusetts

Left: The new Essex-*class carrier* Lexington (CV-16), *part of the famous Task Force 38.*
Below: The original Lexington (CV-2), *with its enormous funnel and the enclosed or 'hurricane' bow, unique to this ship and her sister the* Saratoga (CV-37)

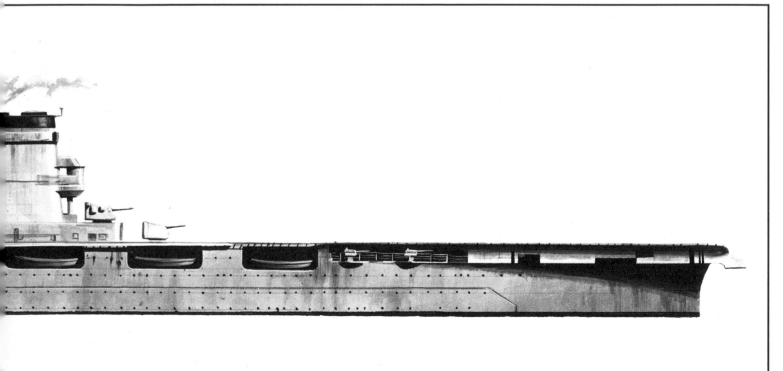

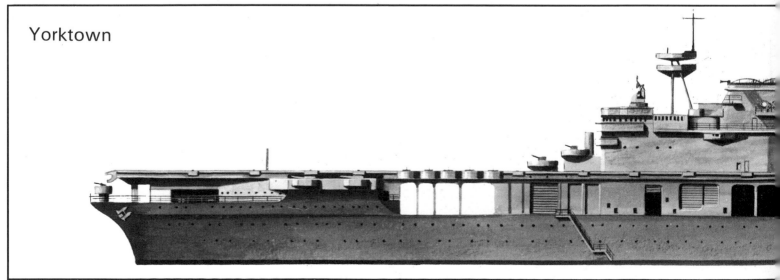

Yorktown

After the not altogether successful experiment in minimum dimensions and fighting qualities of the design of the *Ranger* came the much more balanced *Yorktown* class. All three played a vital part in the desperate fighting of the early days of the war in the Pacific. Two, *Hornet* and *Yorktown*, were lost, and only *Enterprise* survived the war.

Hornet was launched four years after the other two to a slightly modified design, the chief feature of which was an enlarged flight deck, later fitted to the *Enterprise* as well. The basic design of all three was a good well-balanced one; though aircraft capacity was no greater than the *Ranger*'s, on their bigger displacement they could make nearly five knots more speed. Armament, protection and machinery installation were all better. Visually they were distinguished by having a large funnel which was, however, considerably smaller than that of the *Lexington* class.

Like all the earlier American carriers their flight deck was a weak spot, with its wooden planking and complete lack of armour. However, they were sturdily built ships, and both *Hornet* and *Yorktown* took a considerable amount of damage before sinking. Perhaps the most famous individual exploit was the Doolittle Raid on Tokyo. In this a force of twin-engined B-25 army bombers took off from the *Hornet*, larger and heavier aircraft than had ever done so from a carrier before.

YORKTOWN
Displacement 19,800 tons (20,117 tonnes) standard, 25,500 tons (25,909 tonnes) full load
Length 809 feet 6 inches (246 m 73 cm)
Beam 109 feet (33 m 22 cm) (across flight deck)
Draught 21 feet 9 inches (6 m 63 cm)
Machinery 4-shaft geared steam turbines, 120,000 shp = 33 knots
Armour belt: 2½ to 4 inches (63 to 102 mm). deck: 1 to 3 inches (25 to 76 mm)
Guns 8 × 5-inch (127-mm) AA, 4 × 4-barrelled 1.1-inch (28-mm) AA mountings
Aircraft 81 (3 catapults)
Torpedo Tubes none
Launched 4 April 1936 by Newport News Shipbuilding Co.

Top: The original Yorktown (CV-5) *seen during her hectic 48-hour repair which enabled her to surprise the Japanese at Midway. Left: The new* Yorktown (CV-10), *an Essex-class carrier, also served with distinction in the Pacific in operations against the Gilbert Islands, Kwajalein, Truk, Hollandia, the Marianas and Iwo Jima. Below: The first* Yorktown (CV-5)

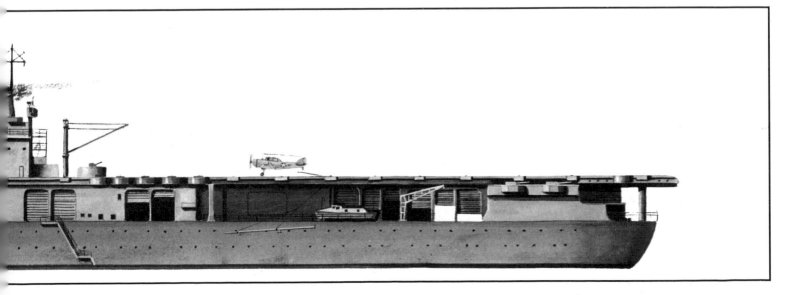

Because of the total carrier tonnage limitations of the Washington Naval Treaty the next American carrier after *Yorktown* and *Enterprise* had to be built to a much reduced tonnage, not much greater than the *Ranger*'s. Like her she suffered from less speed, inferior armament, less protection (though better than the *Ranger*'s), and a smaller operational radius. As one might expect, her aircraft capacity did not suffer, and in one respect, she improved on her predecessors, for she was fitted with the first deck-edge lift. This innovation increased the American lead in the speed and efficiency with which aircraft could be moved from hangar to flight deck and back. However, a deck-edge lift really required the American pattern of open hangar, and would have proved difficult to combine with the British closed armoured box hangars.

Wasp was a little small for full efficiency and the design was not repeated. She was visually quite distinctive, with her tall thin funnel. After proving very useful helping the British ferry fighters to Malta, she was moved to the Pacific where she was lost through submarine attack.

Having tried a range of sizes and types of carriers the Americans very sensibly used their experience to design a standard type of carrier which was built in large numbers throughout the war. This was the excellent *Essex* type, which was not hampered, like the earlier vessels, by treaty limitations. The ships were large, but their increase in size was used to improve their ability to operate larger and heavier aircraft rather than to increase aircraft numbers. There was also an

increase in the 'ship' qualities of the class. Armour was fitted to both flight and hangar decks, though the flight deck was still planked and the sides of the hangar were left unarmoured and vulnerable. The heavy anti-aircraft armament of 5-inch (127-mm) guns was strengthened, but was not as well disposed as that in British ships, nor could it engage as many targets as there were only two director towers. Hull protection was good, as these ships were well subdivided.

Improvements and alterations were constantly being made to the basic design, of which 24 ships, excluding cancelled units, were built. The names of the *Yorktown*, *Hornet*, *Wasp* and *Lexington* were preserved by being given to *Essex*-class ships which were on the stocks when

WASP
Displacement 14,700 tons (14,935 tonnes) standard, 21,000 tons (21,337 tonnes) full load
Length 741 feet 3 inches (225 m 93 cm)
Beam 109 feet (33 m 22 cm) across flight deck
Draught 20 feet (6 m 9 cm)
Machinery 4-shaft geared steam turbines, 75,000 shp = $29\frac{1}{2}$ knots
Armour belt: 4 inches (102 mm). deck: $1\frac{1}{2}$ inches (38 mm)
Guns 8 × 5-inch (127-mm) AA, 4 × 4-barrelled 1.1-inch (28-mm) AA mountings
Aircraft 84 (four catapults)
Launched 4 April 1939 by Bethlehem Shipyard, Quincy

Top: The carrier Wasp *(CV-7) ablaze after being hit by a torpedo at Guadalcanal. Right:* Wasp *in 1942, showing her camouflage scheme*

Wasp

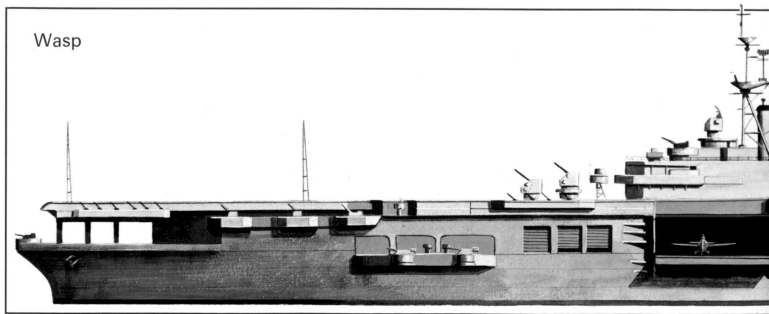

the original bearers of the names were sunk.

The *Essex*-class ships were to be the mainstay of the American carrier arm for long after the war, but a class of three much larger ships, named *Midways*, were building at the end of the war, amalgamating much of what was best in British carrier design with American practice.

While the larger ships of the *Essex* class were still being built, a distressingly large proportion of the United States carrier force was sunk in the early months of the Pacific War. There was an urgent need for rapidly produced stopgaps, of finding a way to get extra flight decks into operation as soon as possible. A satisfactory answer was found in converting nine incomplete hulls of *Cleveland*-class light cruisers to *Independence*-class carriers.

To take the comparatively wide flight deck the narrow cruiser hull had to be bulged. Despite the cramped nature of these conversions they performed well in action, and most important of all they were ready when needed. They could only carry half the aircraft complement of other American carriers, but were a vital reinforcement at a critical time, and an intelligent and well-carried-out improvisation.

Although the *Independence* class originally included four 5-inch (127-mm) guns, these were later removed, and like the British vessels the American ships were left with a battery composed entirely of weapons of 40 mm or less.

At the end of the war another two light carriers, the *Saipan* class, were completed. These were based on the design of the *Baltimore*-class heavy cruisers, but the hulls were specially built, not converted, and were of slightly larger dimensions

INDEPENDENCE
Displacement 11,000 tons (11,176 tonnes) standard, 15,100 tons (15,342 tonnes) full load
Length 622 feet 6 inches (207 m 46 cm)
Beam 109 feet 3 inches (36 m 38 cm) over flight deck
Draught 20 feet (6 m 61 cm)
Machinery 4-shaft geared steam turbines, 100,000 shp = 32 knots
Armour belt: 1½ to 5 inches (38 to 127 mm). deck: 2 to 3 inches (51 to 76 mm)
Guns 4 × 5-inch (127-mm) AA, 26 × 40-mm AA, 40 × 20-mm AA
Aircraft 45 (2 catapults)
Launched 22 August 1942 by New York Shipbuilding Co., Camden

Above: An Independence-*class carrier under air attack. Right:* Independence (CVL-22) *in San Francisco Bay in July 1943. The light cruiser hull is clearly visible, with the four short funnels on the starboard side. Although small and cramped, these hurried conversions acted as useful stopgaps until the* Essex *class were available in quantity. Their high speed made them more useful than the escort carriers and so they remained with the fast carrier task forces in the Central Pacific until 1945. The drawing shows the original 5-inch (127-mm) guns forward and aft of the island and funnels; these guns were removed during the war*

Independence

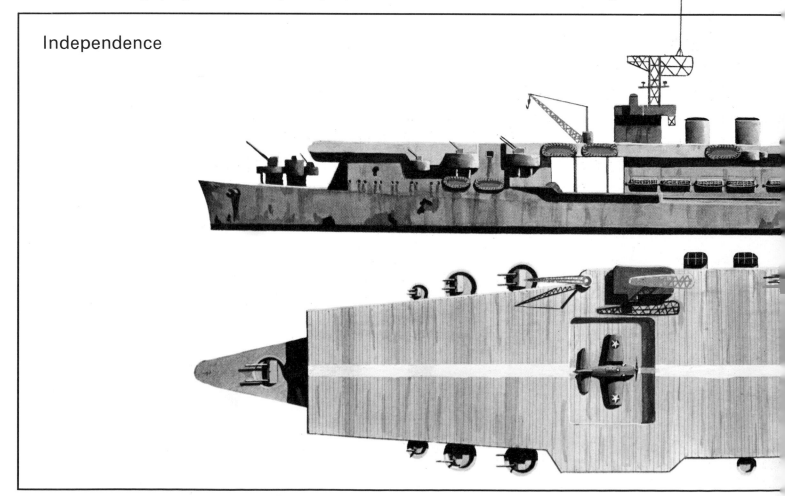

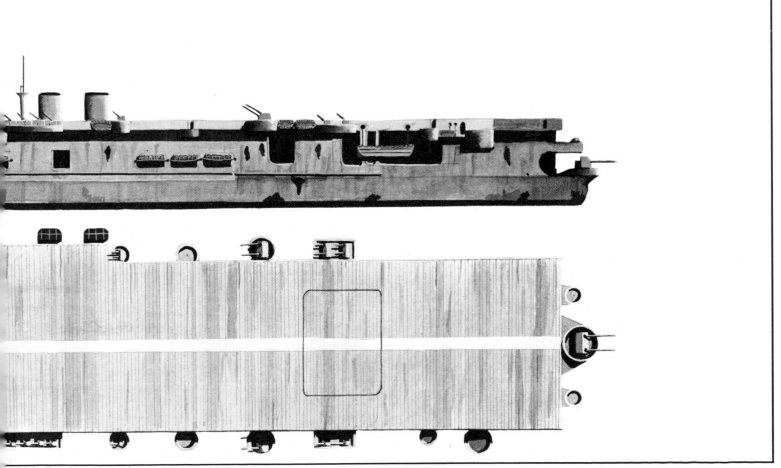

111

than the *Independence* class. They were not quite as cramped as the *Independence* class, but suffered from the same problems of space.

As we have already seen, the British converted the first escort carrier from a German merchantman. However, it was the Americans who built the vast majority of the large number of vessels of this type which served the Allied cause well. The first to appear from American yards were the six converted merchant ships of the *Long Island* class, one for the US Navy, another used by the USN mainly for training British pilots, and four for the Royal Navy. They were slightly more advanced versions of the *Audacity*, with one major improvement in the form of a lift and a hangar for the aircraft.

The 21 *Bogue*-class vessels were all conversions from merchant ships as well, but unlike the earlier motor vessels were all turbine-powered. They also had bigger hangars and an improved anti-aircraft armament. Ten of these useful vessels were retained by the USN, the other eleven lease-lent to Britain. So far all the conversions had been from dry cargo ships, but the US Navy had acquired four brand-new fast oil tankers which appeared to be suitable for conversion, and these became the *Sangamon* class. They had twin screws powered by geared turbines, and were about 60 feet (15.2 m) longer than the other conversions.

Because of this extra size they were the most impressive of the conversions, having extra aircraft capacity, two lifts and two catapults. Instead of exhausting up a funnel on the deck-edge, the boiler gases escaped through ducts at flight deck level aft. The usual two single 5-inch (127-mm) guns were carried aft, and a standard outfit of 40-mm and 20-mm guns, which grew in numbers as the war drew to its close.

The *Sangamon* class were highly successful, being equal in most respects except speed to the *Independence* class of light carriers. Like many of the other Pacific escort carriers they were used more for providing support to landing forces with bombers and fighters than for escorting convoys or carrying anti-submarine aircraft. The respect given to the *Sangamon* class is indicated by the fact that the last wartime escort carriers, the *Commencement Bay* class, were virtually updated copies, but few were in service before the war ended.

To return to the sequence of escort carrier classes, the first escort carriers built from the keel up, though of similar mercantile-type hulls to the conversions, were the 24 ships of the *Prince William* class, of which all except the name ship were transferred to the Royal Navy. All 50 ships of the *Casablanca* class, which had reciprocating steam engines instead of turbines, were kept by the USN. The numbers in which these ships were turned out are almost unbelievable, as are the building times. The chief yard making them finally got the construction time down to three and a half months.

Before leaving American carriers the two oddest should be mentioned. Very sensibly, much decklanding training was done in the safe environment of the Great Lakes, where the only two paddle aircraft carriers in the world were based. These were the converted sidewheel passenger steamers *Sable* and *Wolverine* and they did much useful work despite their bizarre appearance.

The escort carrier Sangamon *runs her trials before entering service in November 1942. Like other escort carriers she has a small bridge and light anti-aircraft guns in sponsons at the edge of the flight deck. The outline of the original fleet oiler hull can be seen below the flight deck, with the machinery aft. The protruding sponson under the flight deck aft is the starboard 5-inch (127-mm) gun position. The drawing below shows the wooden flight deck with its restricted area for landing, the deck-level ducts used in place of funnels to dispose of exhaust gases, and the two aircraft lifts which made this class particularly suitable for flying operations. This enabled them to be used as fleet carriers when they first entered service*

SANGAMON
Displacement 11,400 tons (11,583 tonnes) standard, 24,275 tons (24,664 tonnes) full load
Length 553 feet (168 m 54 cm)
Beam 114 feet 3 inches (34 m 81 cm) across flight deck
Draught 32 feet (9 m 75 cm) maximum
Machinery 2-shaft geared steam turbines, 13,500 shp = 18 knots
Armour none
Guns 2 × 5-inch (127-mm) AA, 8 × 40-mm AA, 12 × 20-mm AA
Aircraft 30 (2 catapults)
Launched 4 November 1939 (as *Esso Trenton*)

Sangamon

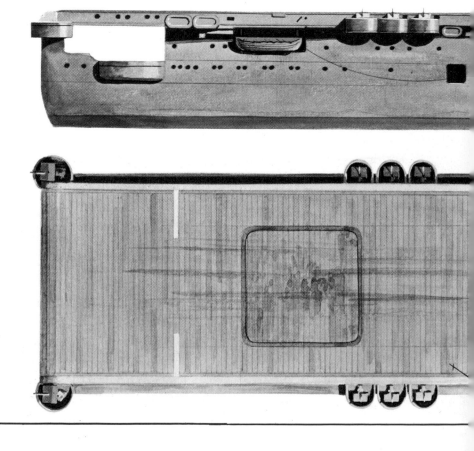

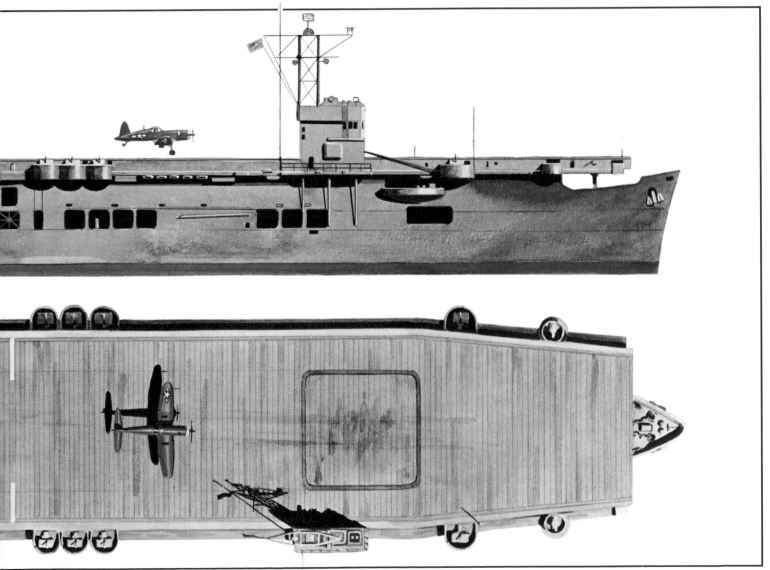

Capital Ships

The Americans, like the British, Italians and Japanese, fought the war with a battleship force partly composed of heavily rebuilt older vessels and partly of new ships. Most of the time the old and the new vessels were used as heavy anti-aircraft escorts for the carriers and as shore-bombardment ships, rather than for their traditional purpose of fighting other ships. The only incident in the Pacific War in which numbers of battleships engaged each other in a surface action was the Battle of Surigao Strait, part of the enormous Battle of Leyte Gulf, and ironically it was the older American battleships which took part, the ones that were meant to stick to the job of shore bombardment. They won an overwhelming victory, mainly because of their use of radar, which had reversed the early Japanese superiority in night fighting.

The oldest American battleships in service during the war were the two ships of the *Wyoming* class. The name ship of the class had been partly disarmed before the war; she was being used as a training ship, like the British *Iron Duke*, and could no longer be considered as a member of the battleship fleet. Her sister, *Arkansas*, retained her twelve 12-inch (305-mm) guns, though she lost her secondary battery of 5-inch (127-mm). Equipped with a new and more powerful anti-aircraft armament of 3-inch (76-mm) and lighter guns, she gave good service throughout the war.

The next class of battleship, consisting of *New York* and *Texas*, were broadly similar to the *Wyoming* except in having ten 14-inch (356-mm) guns. As a result of a quarrel between the Navy Department and the American suppliers of turbines they were unusual in reverting to reciprocating engines for their propulsion. The result of this was that the suppliers lowered their turbine prices to a reasonable standard, and the ships themselves proved to have a reasonable performance despite their old-fashioned machinery. Both were altered like the *Arkansas* during the war, losing their antiquated casemate secondary armament for a better anti-aircraft outfit. The *Arkansas* had the elevation of her 12-inch (305-mm) guns increased for extra range, and similar alterations were made to these two ships' 14-inch (356-mm) turrets.

The US Navy had tended to favour heavy protection for all its battleships, preferring sturdy seaworthy ships with a good armament to faster ships with less armour. With the *Nevada* class (consisting of the name ship and the *Oklahoma*, which latter was sunk at Pearl Harbor) it took a decisive step forward in the technique of warship protection. This was the development of the method of armouring known as 'all or nothing', the logical principle that it was pointless to cover ships with medium or thin armour which could be penetrated by heavy shells, and might do more harm than good. Instead only the most vital points should be protected by armour, and that armour should be as thick as possible. These ships appeared at the beginning of the First World War, and their method of armouring was soon adopted by other powers. Like the previous class both ships had ten 14-inch (356-mm) guns, but these were disposed in two twin and two triple turrets, instead of the five twin turrets of the earlier ships.

Nevada survived Pearl Harbor but was considerably rebuilt, having all the Second World War modifications of the earlier classes, and a new secondary battery of twin 5-inch (127-mm) dual-purpose guns added.

Of the two ships of the next battleship class, one, USS *Arizona*, was sunk at Pearl Harbor, where her wreck remains, but the other, *Pennsylvania*, had the usual wartime conversion like the *Nevada* with a new 5-inch (127-mm) turreted secondary battery. Basically enlarged versions of the earlier class, the *Pennsylvania* and her sister carried two more 14-inch (356-mm) guns by having all the guns in triple turrets; they also had slightly thicker armour, and improved underwater protection.

The one American battleship illustrated is one of a class of three older battleships less altered by reconstruction during the war, though only because they had been extensively rebuilt earlier. The reason for three ships in the class rather than the more usual two was that the United States Navy had just obtained a windfall of cash by selling off two old non-standard pre-dreadnoughts to the Greeks, the *Mississippi* and *Idaho*. As a result of this sale the two names were transferred to two new ships. The third was named after *New Mexico*, which had just attained statehood. The *New Mexico* class differed from their predecessors in having a clipper instead of a ram bow, increased protection and a new and more powerful mark of 14-inch (356-mm) gun. While the ships were building the casemated 5-inch (127-mm) guns were moved up a deck and placed on the forecastle deck, a much more sensible position as they were less likely to be affected by spray. *New Mexico* herself had an experimental form of machinery, turbo-electric propulsion, but this, though not unsatisfactory, was replaced during her rebuilding.

All three of the class were rebuilt in the early 1930s. The enormous lattice masts, hitherto the trade mark of all American battleships, were removed (most of the other older battleships did not lose theirs until after the beginning of the war). They were also reboilered and had a new and much larger bridge structure fitted. Aircraft catapults were added, and extra anti-aircraft guns.

The lack of a major Second World War modernization for these ships can be explained by their absence from Pearl Harbor when the Japanese struck. However, all three ships had powerful 40-mm and 20-mm anti-aircraft batteries added, *Idaho* being the only one to have her original 5-inch (127-mm) replaced by single turreted mounts. To compensate for the additional weight one of the catapults was removed.

These ships make an interesting contrast with the British *Queen Elizabeth* class, with a larger number of lighter guns, less speed but rather better protection. Though they did not play as spectacular a part in the war as their British equivalents they were still powerful and reliable ships.

The *New Mexico* class were completed towards the end of the First World War, and the first post-war ships were the *California* and *Tennessee*.

They were powered by the same type of turbo-electric installation as had been fitted to the *New Mexico*, and were otherwise like their predecessors, but different in appearance as they had twin funnels. Both were damaged at Pearl Harbor, and after this a major rebuilding changed their appearance completely. The twin funnels became one, and the 14-inch (356-mm) guns were the only part of the armament which was not changed.

The *Tennessee* class were followed by the four ships of the *Colorado* class, in which twin 16-inch (406-mm) turrets were substituted for the triple 14-inch (356-mm) of the earlier ships. One ship of the class was never completed because of the Washington Naval Treaty; the other three were rebuilt to a varying extent during the Second World War.

The Washington Treaty caused an entire class of six 16-inch (406-mm)-gunned battleships to be cancelled and scrapped on the slipways. Another class of six ships was also never completed, America's first and last attempt to

MISSISSIPPI
Displacement 33,000 tons (33,529 tonnes) standard, 35,100 tons (35,743 tonnes) full load
Length 624 feet (190 m 19 cm)
Beam 106 feet 3 inches (35 m 38 cm) (over bulges)
Draught 29 feet 3 inches (8 m 91 cm)
Machinery 4-shaft geared steam turbines, 40,000 shp = 21½ knots
Armour belt: 8 to 14 inches (203 to 356 mm). deck: 4 to 6 inches (102 to 152 mm). turrets: 8 to 18 inches (203 to 456 mm)
Guns 12 × 14-inch (356-mm), 12 × 5-inch (127-mm), 8 × 5-inch (127-mm) AA, 3 × 4-barrelled 1.1-inch (28-mm) AA mountings
Torpedo Tubes none
Launched 25 January 1917 by Newport News Shipbuilding Co.

Mississippi (BB-41) *in 1934, just after modernization; she has catapults on 'X' turret and on the stern*

Mississippi

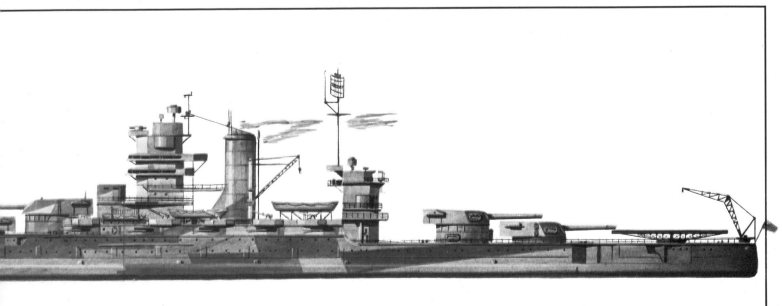

Above: The massive foremast and control top of a battleship blaze at Pearl Harbor. Above right: California (BB-44), *another victim. Below right: The powerful, broad-beamed* South Dakota (BB-57) *on trial*

build battle-cruisers. This aberration was fortunately brought to an end by the treaty, though two of the hulls were put to a more sensible use, and became the aircraft carriers *Lexington* and *Saratoga*.

By the time America launched her next class of two battleships, the *North Carolina* group, the Second World War had broken out, though America was not yet involved. They were not quite as fast as most of their foreign contemporaries, but their 28 knots was a great advance on the 21 knots of their predecessors. Their protection was sound, while the main armament of the three triple 16-inch (406-mm) turrets and secondary dual-purpose twin 5-inch (127-mm) turrets were impressive. It was a pity that the Americans' choice for a light anti-aircraft weapon was the unreliable 1.1-inch (30-mm) gun, but fortunately by the time of Pearl Harbor these weapons were already being replaced by license-built Bofors and Oerlikons.

The four ships of the *South Dakota* class followed the *North Carolinas*, of which they were shorter and broader versions. They were excellent vessels with particularly good underwater protection. Because of their extra beam they needed more power to reach the same speed, but all in all they epitomized the virtues of the American approach to battleship design, and justified their promise in action.

116

After the dumpy, pyramidical single-funnelled *South Dakota* class came the handsome and impressive *Iowa* class with their two large funnels. Six ships were ordered but only four were completed by 1945. With the British *Vanguard* they represent the last generation of battleships. Yet compared with both the British ship and preceeding American classes they seem to be rather poor bargains. Their armament, except in light anti-aircraft guns, was no better than the *South Dakotas*'. To obtain the extremely high theoretical speed of 33 knots they had to devote an enormous amount of space to machinery, and also had to be nearly 200 feet (60.9 m) longer than the *South Dakota* ships. Yet in bad weather the smaller British *Vanguard*, theoretically considerably slower, could easily keep pace with the American giants at a speed of 29.5 knots because of her more seaworthy hull. The British ship had thicker armour, particularly on the decks, where it was most needed, than any American capital ship, and this protection was at least as well disposed. Because of the *Iowa* ships' length their protection was worse than that of the *South Dakota* class and much thinner than most published figures indicate. The story that a greatly improved type of armour was used was just an attempt to conceal this comparative weakness. This is not to say that these American ships were poor designs; they were useful and formidable fighting ships, and certainly a better executed design than that of the *Yamato* class, but they do not compare in technical excellence to the *Vanguard* or the *South Dakota* vessels, despite the first ship's old guns or the latters' lack of speed.

Cruisers

The American habit of building powerful, battle-worthy and unspectacular warships can be seen to advantage in cruiser designs, though some of the heavy cruisers appearing at the end of the war were in fact very spectacular indeed, the largest and most powerful vessels of their kind to be built anywhere. Unlike most other powers the United States did not believe in arming cruisers with torpedoes. The only classes to carry these weapons in the Second World War were the oldest, the *Omaha*, and the lightest, the *Atlanta*. The Japanese went entirely the other way, and their cruisers did well with the fearsome 'Long Lance' torpedo. American cruisers relied on their gun-fire, and the USN developed a rapid-fire drill which relied on getting the maximum amount of shells in the air as soon as possible, in contrast to most other navies which relied on more deliberate salvoes with time allowed for the fall of shot to be observed before the next shells were fired.

America had no cruisers left over from the First World War, when most of her ships of this type had been somewhat elderly armoured cruisers. Just after that war successful British and German light cruiser designs induced the Americans to build their own 6-inch (152-mm) ships. However, the *Omaha* class owed little otherwise to outside influences. They were four-funnelled, and had a twin turret forward and aft. This was reasonable enough, but the other eight 6-inch (152-mm) guns were in extraordinary archaic double-decked casemates. Protection was not impressive, and stability likewise, so half the ships sacrificed a couple of their guns to save on topweight. They were not altered much during the war, presumably because they were not worth it.

No more American cruisers were produced until the end of the 1920s. Then, despite treaty restrictions, the designers produced much more reasonable vessels, the *Pensacola* and *Salt Lake City*. Thanks to great care being taken in saving weight, these ships were 900 tons (914 tonnes) under the limit, despite carrying ten 8-inch (203-mm) guns, two twin and two triple turrets. Protection and speed were both adequate. The US Navy had to some extent reaped the benefit of the latecomer, as all the other major navies had already produced their first treaty cruisers; mistakes could be avoided and innovations copied. One respect in which these American ships were unusual was in carrying the large number of four aircraft. Although the ships originally carried torpedoes these were later removed in favour of extra anti-aircraft guns. One of the worst features of the *Pensacola* class was their low freeboard, but they were very steady ships because of their high centre of gravity. This made them more comfortable but less stable and hence more likely to capsize, but less prone to rolling than ships with lower centres of gravity, such as the next American class, or the British 'Counties'. The American naval architects were much more tolerant of topweight and less rigorous about questions of stability than their British opposite numbers.

The next American class, the *Northampton* series, had a forecastle deck to improve the free-board forward, and saved weight by carrying nine guns in triple turrets.

The *Northampton* class were followed by the *Indianapolis* and her sister *Portland*, which were very like their predecessors. They had better protection: the armoured side belt was in fact less extensive than in previous classes, only covering the machinery spaces, but it was thicker, and the armoured decks were also thickened. These were not particularly attractive-looking ships, with a rather squat silhouette and the after turret too close to the stern for balance. However, warships are not designed to look attractive but to be battleworthy, and these ships were certainly better-balanced designs than the earlier French and Italian treaty cruisers, and better armed than the 'Counties'. The *Portland* class were the first American cruisers to omit torpedo tubes from the start.

PENSACOLA

Displacement 9,100 tons (9,246 tonnes) standard, 12,050 tons (12,243 tonnes) full load
Length 585 feet 9 inches (178 m 53 cm)
Beam 65 feet 3 inches (19 m 88 cm)
Draught 16 feet 3 inches (4 m 95 cm)
Machinery 4-shaft geared steam turbines, 107,000 shp = $32\frac{1}{2}$ knots
Armour belt: 3 inches (76 mm). deck: 1 to 2 inches (25 to 51 mm). turrets: $1\frac{1}{2}$ inches (38 mm)
Guns 10 × 8-inch (203-mm), 8 × 5-inch (127-mm) AA
Aircraft 4 float-planes (2 catapults)
Launched 25 April 1929 by New York Navy Yard

The heavy cruiser Pensacola *(CA-24), the first of the US Washington Treaty cruisers, seen early in the war. Her tripod mainmast has been replaced by a light pole mast*

Pensacola

The design of this class was carried on with minor alterations in the eight ships of the *New Orleans* class, held by many to be the best of the 'treaty cruisers' of any nation except the French *Algérie*. They differed from the earlier class in having improved protection, better distributed, and in having a longer forecastle deck.

The next group, the large 6-inch (152-mm) *Brooklyn* class, were designed as a reaction to the Japanese *Mogami*, with a similar arrangement of five triple turrets. Their protection was only slightly reduced from that of the *New Orleans* class, and although called light cruisers they were much the same size and tonnage as their 8-inch (203-mm) predecessors. Their appearance was, however, completely different not only because of the layout of the turrets, but also because of their flush deck and high freeboard. Like many other American ships they gave the impression of being a hull on which assorted oddments of superstructure and armament had been piled, rather than a ship designed as a whole.

An unusual feature was the aircraft hangar under the quarter-deck complete with lift to serve the stern catapults. This was in fact a questionable feature, as any large compartment aft is dangerous to the ship's watertight integrity. It was never repeated in other American ships despite rumours that the later battleships had stern hangars. One has only to look at the numbers of photographs of storm-damaged Kingfisher float-planes to realize that these aircraft were stowed on deck.

Above left: The heavy cruiser Indianapolis *(CA-35) in March 1939. Below left: The light cruiser* Cleveland *(CL-55) just after the war. She has dual-purpose 5-inch (127-mm) guns in twin turrets, a great improvement in anti-aircraft firepower. In all 29 were built to this design and a further nine were converted to* Independence-*class carriers*

The next design, the USS *Wichita*, although called a 'modified *New Orleans*' was really a *Brooklyn* with three triple 8-inch (203-mm) turrets. The *Brooklyn* design was further modified, losing one 6-inch (152-mm) turret but adding to the anti-aircraft armament, to produce the *Cleveland* class. Twenty-seven of these powerful ships were built as cruisers, three were cancelled, and, as we have already seen, nine became aircraft carriers. This was numerically the largest cruiser class ever built – yet another example of the extraordinary capacity of US industry. The *Baltimore* class were basically 8-inch (203-mm) versions of the *Cleveland*, and undoubtedly the best heavy cruisers of their time, neither their German nor Japanese contemporaries being a match in power or balance of qualities. Heavy cruisers seem to have been a favourite American type, and certainly the Americans showed particular aptitude in designing them.

New classes of enormous 6-inch (152-mm) and 8-inch (203-mm) cruisers were being completed as the war drew to an end. Only two ships of the *Fargo* class of 6-inch (152-mm) ships were built, single-funnelled developments of the *Cleveland* vessels. The single funnel was to allow a better distribution of the anti-aircraft armament, which by this stage of the war was reaching enormous proportions in all American heavy units. The *Baltimore* design was modified in a similar way to produce the *Oregon City*, and this class itself was improved and enlarged to become the *Des Moines* class. The first two of this class were laid down just before the war ended, and they were armed with fully automatic 8-inch (203-mm) gun mountings.

They were nearly as formidable as the *Alaska* and *Guam*, two odd vessels which were designed to counter a rumoured Japanese class of very heavy cruisers which never materialized. To counter these imaginary vessels the American class had nine 12-inch (305-mm) guns in triple turrets. Despite this armament it would be wrong to think of them as battle-cruisers or capital ships of any kind, like the *Scharnhorst* or *Dunkerque*. They were instead just exceptionally large and well-armed cruisers, enlarged versions of the *Baltimore* class. They turned out in the event to be useful escorts for carriers thanks to their high speed and powerful anti-aircraft battery but were very costly to run.

To move from the largest cruisers to the smallest, mention must be made of two wartime classes of cruisers armed with 5-inch (127-mm) guns. These were the *Atlanta* class and an improved version, the *Oakland* class. The first-mentioned had a total of eight twin 5-inch (127-mm) turrets, reduced to six in the later class, which also had fewer torpedo tubes and more light anti-aircraft weapons. Their *raison d'être* is a little elusive; although their armament was excellent for anti-aircraft purposes, there were too few directors to take advantage of it, and they were a little large to integrate well with flotillas of destroyers while having a gun which was not heavy enough to give a decisive superiority over a large enemy destroyer. Perhaps the Americans were just not at home in designing light as opposed to heavy cruisers.

INDIANAPOLIS

Displacement 9,950 tons (10,109 tonnes) standard, 12,575 tons (12,776 tonnes) full load
Length 610 feet 3 inches (186 m)
Beam 66 feet (20 m 11 cm)
Draught 17 feet 3 inches (5 m 25 cm)
Machinery 4-shaft geared steam turbines, 107,000 shp = 32¾ knots
Armour belt: 3 to 4 inches (76 to 102 mm). deck: 2 inches (51 mm). turrets: 1½ to 3 inches (38 to 76 mm)
Guns 9 × 8-inch (203-mm), 8 × 5-inch (127-mm) AA, 4 × 4-barrelled 1.1-inch (28-mm) AA
Aircraft 4 (2 catapults)
Launched 7 November 1931 by New York Shipbuilding Co., Camden

Indianapolis

Destroyers

Johnston

American destroyers had two great advantages. One was their standard gun armament which consisted of the superb 5-inch (127-mm) weapon. This was the best destroyer gun of the war, equally effective in low-angle and high-angle fire; it fired a respectable weight of shell at a good rate, and was easy to man. The second advantage was that by the time America entered the Second World War she had developed a reliable high-pressure steam plant, which gave economy and performance without the frequent breakdowns that German ships suffered. As a result the standard wartime destroyers were probably the best large destroyers in the world, besides being the most numerous. Thanks to the excellent fleet train, the Americans could rely on refuelling at sea rather than excessively large bunkers to cope with the immense distances of the Pacific, but even so their ships had an impressive radius of action.

Part of this excellence was possibly due to the fact that the Americans started their interwar destroyer development with an inadequate design, and built a whole range of types in the 1930s which gave them a chance to experiment with different arrangements of size and characteristics. Once war came they could standardize on one excellent type and mass-produce it. This was in direct contrast to the British, who had begun with excellent design and had by and large stuck to it in the interwar years, but then did far more chopping and changing of their standard design during the war.

For years after the First World War the Americans built no destroyers. They had over-produced enormous numbers of their standard 'four stacker' design, which compared unfavourably with the contemporary British 'V & W' classes. The disposition of their gun armament, and more especially of their torpedo tubes, was very clumsy and they were exceedingly narrow. Their best features were their good speed and their flush-decked hull, a structurally sounder arrangement than the raised forecastle deck of most other destroyers. Despite their disadvantages the USN had many of these destroyers left at a time when want of fast escort ships was the most pressing need, and both the fifty 'least-lent' to the Royal Navy and those retained by the USN performed valuable work. They underwent many conversions, to long-range escorts, fast transports, destroyer minesweepers, and seaplane tenders.

It was not until 1932 that America laid down any more destroyers, the *Farragut* class, which were not unlike the British interwar flotilla leaders, with five 5-inch (127-mm) guns and a raised forecastle, but possessing slightly greater size and bunker capacity. Like their British contemporaries these vessels appeared a little small to deal with the super-destroyers being built by France and Italy, and more especially the influential Japanese *Fubuki* class. Like the British 'Tribals' which were also inspired by those Japanese ships, the *Porter* class of flotilla leaders had eight guns in twin turrets, but their anti-aircraft and torpedo armaments were both heavier than the British ships, and as a result these vessels were somewhat overloaded.

The *Mahan* class reverted to the *Farragut* type, except in having three sets of torpedo tubes, the after ones of which were mounted abreast of each other, not an ideal arrangement as each set could only be fired on one side. These destroyers had their guns in a combination of shielded and open mounts, but a modified version of the class mounted the prototype single 5-inch (127-mm) enclosed turret which was to prove such a success. Standard wartime modifications to all ships included the removal of the fifth, midships-mounted 5-inch (127-mm) and the substitution of light anti-aircraft weapons.

The *Gridley* and *Benham* classes increased the torpedo armament further by having two pairs of quadruple tubes. They only carried four 5-inch (127-mm) guns, and were notable for their single funnels. The *Porter* class of flotilla leaders were followed by the five ships of the *Somers* and *Sampson* classes. These had one less twin turret than their predecessors, but carried an extra set of torpedo tubes, and also had a rather ugly single funnel.

With the *Sims* class the USN reverted to a torpedo armament of two sets of quadruple tubes; originally three were to have been fitted, but stability was not adequate. Unlike the earlier classes the aftermost gun as well as the forward ones had a turret, but the other gun aft was still in an open mount.

The next two classes, *Benson* and *Livermore*, returned to two funnels, as they had adopted 'unit' machinery with alternate engine and boiler rooms, which increased the length slightly but made for a better chance of surviving major machinery damage as all the boilers were unlikely to be put out of action at the same time. The large *Bristol* group ordered in 1940 were very similar, except in having four instead of five 5-inch (127-mm) guns, and extra light anti-aircraft guns instead. All the gun mounts were turreted.

JOHNSTON
Displacement 2,050 tons (2,082 tonnes) standard, 2,940 tons (2,987 tonnes) full load
Length 376 feet (114 m 60 cm)
Beam 39 feet 9 inches (12 m 11 cm)
Draught 13 feet 9 inches (4 m 19 cm)
Machinery 2-shaft geared steam turbines, 60,000 shp = 37 knots
Armour none
Guns 5 × 5-inch (127-mm) DP, 10 × 40-mm AA 7 × 20-mm AA
Torpedo Tubes 10 × 21-inch (530-mm)
Launched 25 March 1943 by Seattle-Tacoma Shipbuilding Co.

Above: A typical 'flush-decker' destroyer, Crowninshield (DD-134), *a survivor from World War I which went to the Royal Navy as HMS* Chelsea *in 1940 and to the Soviet Navy as* Derzki *in 1944. Left: The illustration shows the Fletcher-class destroyer* Johnston (DD-557), *which was sunk at the Battle of Leyte Gulf gallantly defending escort carriers from attack by Japanese battleships. These destroyers were built in large numbers as the standard US Navy design of the war, and they proved highly successful*

Allen M Sumner

The standard wartime destroyer design was the *Fletcher* class, of which 24 had been ordered before Pearl Harbor; immediately after that another hundred were contracted for, though not all were completed. This excellent design was an enlarged *Bristol* to take extra anti-aircraft weapons, while carrying five 5-inch (127-mm) guns and ten torpedo tubes. The basic difference from the *Fletcher* class's predecessors was that the hulls were flush-decked, a throwback to the best feature of the 'four stackers'; they also introduced double-reduction geared turbines to give extra economy.

Johnston was one of these fine ships. It will be noticed from her drawing how the American designers were not afraid to place the torpedo tubes high in the ship. They made use of bottom ballast when necessary to counterbalance such high-mounted weights, a step which was anathema to most foreign naval architects and avoided whenever possible. Perhaps the best feature of these ships as compared to the British standard destroyers before the 'Battle' class was that they were large enough to carry an impressive battery of 20-mm and 40-mm guns, very necessary in the Pacific and other theatres of war. Once again the Americans had produced a workmanlike design which did not exaggerate any one characteristic at the expense of others, but instead was a well-balanced and battleworthy type of destroyer.

Three of the class had the extraordinary installation of an aircraft catapult and seaplane in place of the torpedo tubes and one turret. This idea was a bit of a non-starter, as destroyers were too small to operate an aircraft adequately, and in any case there were enough spotting aircraft available in other more suitable vessels.

The *Allen M Sumner* class were adaptations of the *Fletcher* class to take three twin turrets. This turret had already proved its usefulness in larger ships, and the only major alteration necessary to these destroyers was a slight increase in beam. Both torpedo tubes and the anti-aircraft guns had to be redistributed, but otherwise these ships retained the pattern of their predecessors, powerful and well-equipped fighting ships. The only major differences within the class was that one group were built as fast minelayers, with all the torpedo tubes removed and an extra quadruple 40-mm mounting added. A later modification to many of the other members of the class was the substitution of similar 40-mm Bofors mounts for the after bank of torpedo tubes. Like their predecessors the ships of this class were built in large numbers, as were those of the final wartime destroyer class. This was the *Gearing* group, whose only new feature was an extra 14 foot (4.3 m)-long section inserted in the hull.

Both *Gearing* and *Sumner* ships were to be the mainstay of the destroyer force of the USN for

Above: The Allen M. Sumner (DD-692) *was the first of an improved* Fletcher *design put in hand in 1942. The only important differences were a longer hull to allow more fuel and twin 5-inch (127-mm) guns in place of the single mountings. Right: The* Ray (SS-271) *was typical of the* Gato-*class submarines, the standard wartime submarine design*

ALLEN M SUMNER
Displacement 2,200 tons (2,235 tonnes) standard, 3,515 tons (3,571 tonnes) full load
Length 376 feet 6 inches (114 m 75 cm)
Beam 40 feet (12 m 19 cm)
Draught 15 feet 9 inches (4 m 80 cm)
Machinery 2-shaft geared steam turbines, 60,000 shp = 34 knots
Armour none
Guns 6 × 5-inch (127-mm) DP, 12 × 40-mm AA, 8 × 20-mm AA
Torpedo Tubes 10 × 21-inch (530-mm)
Launched 15 December 1943 by Federal Shipbuilding Co., Kearny

many years after the war. Eventually some of them were modernized and rebuilt, with helicopter facilities in some cases, and with new weapons and electronic equipment. Only now are they finally going out of service. having served long and valiantly in various guises, just as their four-funnelled First World War predecessors.

Submarines

Few realize that the American submarine arm waged the only completely successful submarine offensive – that US submarines succeeded where the U-boats failed – in completely strangling the lifelines of a maritime nation. If the atomic bomb had never been dropped, Japan was already doomed to defeat because the ships which brought essential supplies had nearly all been sunk. Though aircraft, surface ships, mines (many laid by American submarines) and British and Dutch submarines had all played their part, the lion's share of sunken Japanese tonnage was claimed by US submarines.

Much of this success was due to the incredible failure of Japan for most of the war to take adequate precautions to defend her commerce. This was a blunder only matched by an equally unbelievable failure to use the large and well-equipped Japanese submarine force against American and Allied shipping, which provided the essential logistic support for the war in the Pacific. Much of the success, however, was due to the high quality of American submarines and submariners; despite the Japanese doctrine of concentrating their submarines on the task of sinking enemy warships, it was the Americans who achieved a much higher total of enemy ships sunk by submarines. The American success in undersea warfare is even more creditable when it is realized that American submarine torpedoes (like German) had a shocking record of malfunctions in the early months of the war. It took nearly a year of the Pacific war before the Americans had an adequately lethal and reliable weapon for their boats.

Even more than the carriers and destroyers the American wartime standard submarine

design is an example of the process of producing a wide variety of small experimental classes or 'one-off' designs in peacetime, trying them thoroughly over a long period of time, and then combining all the best features in a standard design which can be mass-produced in a hurry.

At the outbreak of the war America had a number of submarines built during or just after the previous conflict. These were the 'O', 'R' and 'S' classes, which were not much use for anything except training; some of the 'R' and 'S' classes were transferred to the Royal Navy for this purpose. One of their chief disadvantages was that they had a totally inadequate range for the Pacific, and it is not surprising that the Americans were so impressed by the large German 'U-cruisers' of the First World War and that they proceeded to adapt the basic design to their own purposes. As the Japanese did exactly the same, it is interesting to see the differences and similarities between the submarines evolved by both nations from this common starting point.

Although the earlier interwar American submarines were initially given numbers prefixed by the letter 'V' it is simpler to refer to them by the fish names they later received. The *Barracuda* and her two sisters were, like most of their successors, large boats, concentrating on range and surface speed rather than the fast diving and underwater performance which was beginning to assume greater importance for most European submarines.

The next submarine built in America was the huge *Argonaut*, fitted with two 6-inch (152-mm) guns and designed as a minelayer. She was followed by two similar boats which were not, however, fitted for minelaying, and carried more

torpedo tubes instead. These, like all the early big American submarines, were powered by the same type of German diesel that had been used by the U-cruisers. Next came the *Dolphin*, a not entirely successful attempt to achieve the best qualities of these big boats on a smaller displacement. The following boats, the *Cachalot* class, reduced size still further, but were rather more successful. Their hulls were welded, a technique of construction in which the Americans were well in the lead, and which gave stronger hulls for less weight.

This class had been a little small but had still shown that 1,500-ton (1,524-tonne) submarines could operate successfully in the Pacific. Their successors, the *Porpoise* class, were slightly larger and introduced one of the most vital components of the future standard wartime submarine. This was a good, reliable, light and powerful home-produced diesel. In fact, as the result of a naval design competition, no fewer than four firms developed successful engines of this kind.

The *Salmon* and *Sargo* classes slightly in-

RAY

Displacement 1,526 tons (1,550 tonnes) surfaced, 2,424 tons (2,462 tonnes) submerged
Length 311 feet 9 inches (95 m)
Beam 27 feet 3 inches (8 m 32 cm)
Draught 15 feet 3 inches (4 m 66 cm)
Machinery surfaced: 2-shaft diesel-electric, 5,400 bhp = 20¼ knots; submerged: 2-shaft electric, 2,740 shp = 8¾ knots
Guns 1 × 3-inch (76-mm) AA, 1 × 40-mm AA
Torpedo Tubes 10 × 21-inch (530-mm)
Launched 28 February 1943 by Manitowoc Shipbuilding Co.

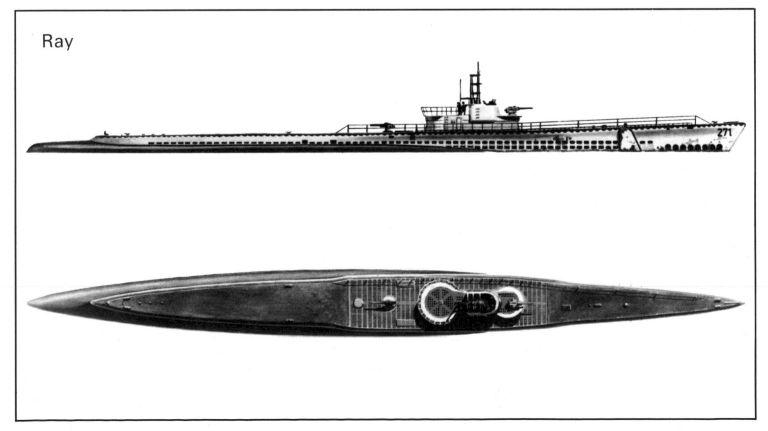

Ray

creased surface speed and torpedo outfit, and had a somewhat complex drive arrangement on the surface, using both geared diesel and diesel-electric drive, except for four which had diesel electric drive. In contrast the next group of classes, the *Tambor* and *Gar* vessels, used direct drive, but these were an aberration from the main line of American submarine development.

The *Gato* class, of which *Ray* was one, had been designed, and the first boats ordered, before America joined the war. The design was adopted as standard, and over 200 were finally ordered. These had the welded hulls, excellent diesels and large torpedo armaments developed in preceeding classes, with the range and high surface speed essential for success in the Pacific. They also had more attention paid to habitability and crew comfort than the submarines of any other nation. This was, admittedly, not saying much, as all submarines, until the advent of nuclear boats well after the end of the war, were notoriously cramped and uncomfortable. None-

theless the greater comfort of American crews did pay dividends by permitting longer patrols. These big boats did not dive as fast or manoeuvre as well underwater as the smaller German or British boats, but they had less need of these evasive tactics. Japanese anti-submarine forces were not as numerous or technically sophisticated as those of the Germans or the Italians (who had quite a good record in anti-submarine operations).

Gun armament varied quite considerably.

The main weapon varied between 3-inch (76-mm), 4-inch (102-mm), or 5-inch (127-mm) calibre, although the latter was the most common type. One or more 20-mm guns were often supplemented by 40-mm ones. Radar gradually became one of the most important parts of the submarine's equipment, and a large proportion of 'kills' were obtained by intelligent use of this device. The later units of the class, from the *Balao* on, were given thicker hulls to enable them to dive deeper, while a new class, the *Tench* group, still changed the basic design very little, as there was no need to alter a type which had proved so ideal for its purpose. After the war new ideas about submarine design came into favour, and many ships of these classes were altered to the new 'Guppy' formula, streamlined for underwater speed and with more powerful electric motors and more battery power. However, the submarines of the *Gato* and *Tench* classes had already done their basic job, the defeat of Japan, very adequately.

Many older submarines and less successful experimental types were used in the humble but essential job of training the enormous numbers of men required for the wartime submarine programmes. Although built in 1933, the Cuttlefish (SS-171) *and her sister* Cachalot (SS-170) *were soon relegated to training duties.* Cuttlefish *is armed with a 3-inch (76-mm) gun abaft the conning tower and a 20-mm anti-aircraft gun, whereas her sister carried the 3-inch gun forward*